GULLAH CUISINE

By Land and by Sea

Harvest Dance, 2000 © Jonathan Green

GULLAH CUISINE

By Land and by Sea

Featuring Gullah Chef Charlotte Jenkins
Narrative by William Baldwin
Artwork by Jonathan Green

Evening Post Publishing Co.
Charleston, South Carolina
EveningPostBooks.com

EVENING
POST
PUBLISHING
COMPANY
Charleston
South Carolina

with Joggling Board Press

Published by
Evening Post Publishing Company
Charleston, South Carolina
EveningPostBooks.com

Editors: Susan Kammeraad-Campbell/ John M. Burbage
Designer: Gill Guerry

First printing 2010
Printed and bound in the USA
by The R.L. Bryan Co.

A CIP catalog record for this book has been applied
for from the Library of Congress.

ISBN: 978-0-9825154-2-6

Cover art:
Red Tomatoes, 1992, oil on canvas, 16" x 20" © Jonathan Green – private collection

All artwork included in this publication is copyrighted by Jonathan Green. Some of the artwork is held by the artist; some is held in private collections.

All photographs are copyrighted by Mic Smith unless otherwise indicated. Photo credits are listed on page 213.

Charlotte Jenkins

Charlotte Jenkins, owner of Gullah Cuisine in Mount Pleasant, South Carolina, is recognized as a premier Gullah chef. Her cooking has been praised by *Southern Living, The New York Times, The Washington Post* and *The Boston Globe.* Jenkins learned to cook Gullah the way her mama, her grandmama and all the mamas who have come before her – by working alongside one another. She also trained at Johnson & Wales University in Charleston where she adapted the traditional recipes to be more healthful. In 1997, she and her husband, Frank, opened Gullah Cuisine.

William P. Baldwin

William P. Baldwin is an award-winning novelist, biographer and historian. A life-long resident of coastal South Carolina, his works include *Plantations of the Low Country; Low Country Plantations Today;* and the oral histories *Mrs. Whaley and her Charleston Garden; Heaven is a Beautiful Place* and *Journey of a Hope Merchant.* Baldwin's novel, *The Hard to Catch Mercy,* won the Lillian Smith Award for fiction. He is married with two grown sons, two wonderful daughters-in-law, three near perfect grandchildren and a kayak. And he's a big, big fan of Lowcountry cooking.

Jonathan Green

Jonathan Green, painter and printmaker, grew up in Gardens Corner in Beaufort County, South Carolina. Green, a graduate of the Art Institute of Chicago, has participated in traveling exhibitions throughout the United States and more than fifty solo exhibitions. Green received an honorary doctorate from the University of South Carolina the same year *Gullah Images: The Art of Jonathan Green* was published. In 2009, Green received the Key of Life Award for his achievements in the visual fine arts from the NAACP. "The Gullah people depicted in Jonathan Green's world look like they got dressed while staring at rainbows," says writer Pat Conroy of Fripp Island, South Carolina.

Mic Smith

Mic Smith, originally from Indiana, came to the Palmetto State in the early 1990s and soon established himself as one of the top photojournalists in the Carolinas. For many years, Smith used a lens to tell stories of the lush Lowcountry and the historic city of Charleston for *The Post and Courier.* In 2007, the newspaper nominated him for a Pulitzer Prize. Smith now works independently through Mic Smith Photography and Lowcountry Photojournalism and lives with his family on the Isle of Palms, a few miles from Gullah Cuisine restaurant. The six-foot-four-inch Hoosier with a legendary appetite savors every visit to Charlotte Jenkins' kitchen.

ACKNOWLEDGEMENTS

It takes a village to create a cookbook. This one has been simmering on the back burner of Charlotte Jenkins' stove for many years. I had the supreme pleasure to be asked to help Charlotte lift the pot off that back burner, move it to the front and turn up the fire. Editing this book has been a journey that has allowed me to go where you will be able to go as a reader – into Charlotte's creative kitchen, but also into her life. Charlotte and her husband, Frank, grew up Gullah at a time when the Old Ways were giving way to the New Ways. In many ways, they have lived the American dream, rising up from humble origins to build a nationally recognized Gullah restaurant where today they would regard being interviewed by *Southern Living, The Washington Post, The New York Times, et al*, as all in a day's work.

As I said, making this book has been a journey that has involved many. The chef, the writer, the editors and I would like to thank those many souls who contributed to this project both directly and indirectly.

Thanks to Dennis T. Comer whose early insights and enthusiasm convinced Charlotte that a cookbook was in her future. Thank you to Marion Sullivan of the Culinary Institute at Trident Technical College, who played matchmaker in finding the right publisher for the book and offered expert guidance. Thank you to the Culinary Institute for bringing Chef Kevin Mitchell to the testing table and thanks to Sysco Food Service. Thanks also to Selden "Bud" Hill of the Village Museum, Dale Rosengarten, Carrie Hirsch, Emmy Bronson and Lil Baldwin. Thank you to Jane Aldridge and Michael Coker at the South Carolina Historical Society; to Richard Weedman for help with Jonathan Green's artwork; to *Charleston Magazine* and photographer Terry Kuzniar for use of the holiday images; to the staff of the Charles Pinckney Center; and to South Carolina Poet Laureate Marjory Wentworth.

Our thanks to U.S. Congressman James Clyburn of South Carolina for his support of legislation that created the Gullah/Geechee Cultural Heritage Corridor. Recently, the National Park Service named a 15-member commission in Charleston, South Carolina, charged with overseeing the implementation of this federally designated corridor from Jacksonville, Florida to Wilmington, North Carolina.

"The story of the Gullah/Geechee people and their contributions to this country began in 1619 when the first Africans arrived at the Jamestown settlement," said Clyburn at the naming of the commission. "After more than seven years of work to establish this corridor, today marks the first day of the hard work this commission will undertake to preserve and share that nearly 400-year history that is the core purpose of this initiative."

The Avery Research Center in Charleston and Penn Center on St. Helena Island, South Carolina, are commended for the work they do in sharing the African-American experience. A special thanks to Emory Campbell, long-time director of Penn Center, now chair of the Gullah/Geechee Cultural Heritage Corridor.

Thanks to Jonathan Green for painting this book colorful; Mic Smith for so artfully capturing a modern Gullah story in photographs. And a special thanks to Pierre Manigault and John M. Burbage of the Evening Post Publishing Company for putting their muscle, expertise and good spirit behind this project; Gill Guerry of *The Post and Courier* for being a design-clairvoyant when it comes to putting on the page what's rattling around in my head; Billy Baldwin, whose steady ways with words and people brought forth this story of the Old Ways and the New; and Charlotte, who so very early in life found cooking to be an expression of love.

– Susan Kammeraad-Campbell, co-editor

Oyster Man, 1998 © Jonathan Green

Chapter One

A WORLD THE GULLAH BUILT

William Baldwin:
A WRITER'S VIEW FROM THE ROOTS UP

The Carolina Lowcountry is a world the Gullah built. Yet the Gullah would be the first to say God made this world, and they are the humblest of wayfarers. "Dear Lord, prop me up in my leaning places," goes their familiar prayer, one that in spirit, at least, has been around for almost four hundred years. You see, the term "Gullah" once referred to a particular tribe or area in Africa, and the natives so named often found their way to the slave auction blocks of Charleston.

Settled in 1670, Charleston was the most tropical of the English colonies. It was considered part of the Caribbean and a place of plantations. Along the coast and twenty miles inland, the land is a watery collection of swamps and rivers where, if much labor were provided, rice could be cultivated. And along the very edge of the ocean is a series of Sea Islands where, if much labor were provided, a luxury quality of cotton could be grown. Hence the early and continued arrival of captive Africans who brought much of their vibrant culture with them.

William Baldwin

LANGUAGE

The pidgin convergence of English, Scots and African dialects used by these early arrivals would through time and isolation evolve into a distinct Gullah language, one still heard today in remote corners. *Okra, juke, biddy* are some of the actual African words still with us. Ethnologists have found evidence of hundreds. But it is in the syntax and the related musical rhythms that the language is most evident. *"Mek so?"* ("Why?") *"E unrabble 'e mout' all day."* ("He talked all day.") Indeed, Gullah's lilting sounds can still be detected in the speech of black and white Lowcountry natives – sometimes referred to as Geechees. As you'll see from their comments, both Charlotte and Frank Jenkins of Gullah Cuisine grew up in this linguistic environment – one even they, at times, met with amusement and frustration.

This is one of the first roadside basket stands on U.S. Highway 17 in Mount Pleasant taken around 1929, about three miles from the present location of Gullah Cuisine.

MUSIC AND THE CHURCH

The joyful, mournful and rhythmic songs of the Lowcountry's black churches have their roots in the African shouts of the slaves' small praise houses. Early on, drums were outlawed in South Carolina out of fear they would be used to send messages of insurrection. And while Christianity was encouraged for all on the plantation, literacy was not. The Bible could be a dangerous book, and hence oral prayer-giving evolved. Part Christian, part African, the Gullah music and prayer that resulted has a richness – one that slipped into even the most secular corners of the world. The dance craze known as the Charleston began as an African religious expression and made its way from the Charleston alleyways to Paris. More to the point, the beach and shag music for which Carolina is famous was an invention of black musicians well-schooled in those African Christian churches. And again you will see that Charlotte and Frank, though modern – even liberal in their religious thought – were well churched as children. And both are fans of what some feel is African America's biggest contribution to the world's music – jazz.

CRAFTS

Evidence of African crafts can still be found in coastal Carolina. Wood carvers, folk-painters, jewelers and quilters all make use of African motifs, but it is the basket making tradition that is the best preserved of these early crafts. Made of thick rushes and palmettos, the earliest baskets were used as household containers and farm implements – the famed rice fanner among them. Following the Civil War, Penn Center near Beaufort worked with some success to maintain this tradition, but a true market developed in a less likely spot. Working with the more delicate sweetgrass and pine straw, women began to sew decorative baskets that they placed in roadside stands just north of Mount Pleasant and sold to tourists as well as locals. This is the very district where Charlotte and Frank established their restaurant.

Today, examples of this distinct basket tradition can be found in museums across the country. "A Six Mile thing," says Charlotte Jenkins – who grew up in the Ten Mile community, four miles past Six Mile – of the craft. She was a school-age friend of Mary Jackson, the most famous basket maker of all. That's not the only craft, however. Modern quilt makers sometimes return to distinct African patterns, and jewelry makers fashion china berries, sea shells and more into distinctive and beautiful necklaces and earrings. Cast net makers are still out there, nimbly moving fingers to create not just fishing nets but family heirlooms. In slavery days, skilled metal workers made decorative ironwork to grace Charleston mansions. In our own time, master craftsman Philip Simmons and his friends and apprentices have carried on this Gullah tradition.

The ironwork of celebrated master craftsman Philip Simmons can be found in and around Charleston.

COOKING

The Gullah cooking tradition extends back at least three hundred years – and much further if we include its African antecedents. To get the most from the least: that's one way to define the process. Rice, corn, potatoes, collards, seafood and pork are basic ingredients, for these were the most dependable crops and the most available meats. And they must be cooked simply, preferably in one pot and maybe two if need be. Cooking for his grandfather's pulpwood crew, a twelve-year-old Frank sometimes risked a third small one for the peas. He had four menus and each one started with rice. Charlotte recalls her mother's blackfish, heads on, wrapped in brown paper and simmered on a rusty sheet of hot tin. This is wood-fire cooking, all of it simply done and in large quantities. Yet, don't be fooled, for the Gullah tradition has a long-standing flexibility. Recipes were borrowed from the French and English, even from the Turks. What works, works. Seasoning is extremely important. And, of course, fried chicken and macaroni were there on Sundays. I won't go further here. You're about to hear much more from the actual chefs.

THE LAND

We live in the world the Gullah made. That's the literal truth. The early planters sought out slaves from the rice-growing regions of Africa because this crop was both tricky and labor intensive. The fields were carved at first from the inland swamps and then the tidal reaches of the river marshes. Both were well forested, well, as in grand stands of mighty cypress trees that had to be destroyed – stumps included.

Then a complex system of waterways and dikes produced the fields, immense fields that, for flooding purposes, had to be level.

The amount of hand labor that went into the Santee Delta fields alone has been compared to the slave labor required to build the three great pyramids of Egypt. Now consider that these fields, long since abandoned to trees and marsh grass, ran all the way from Georgetown to the Savannah River and inland for up to twenty miles, and imagine dozens and dozens of pyramids set upon this countryside – imagine it, each side of U.S. Highway 17 marked by huge triangles of stone. And as the Sea Island cotton, grown as it was on a well-manured soil and tended only by hoes, we may add a dozen more stone monuments along the ocean front. In labor expended, in dirt dug and water courses rerouted, that's the world the Gullah made.

NEIGHBORHOODS

Even more curious was the unintended effect these impoundments had on the patterns of population. From the beginning, the Lowcountry was noted as a dangerous, fever-ridden place to settle, but shortly after the Revolution, an even more virulent form of malaria was introduced – one probably brought from Africa. The carrier, the Anopheles mosquito, bred well in the rice fields and the captive slave population acted as a blood reservoir, for their sickle cell immunity and general sturdiness gave them some protection. From May to November, the white population abandoned the plantations and stayed in small summer communities, places where a sea breeze or absence of swamps kept the malaria at bay.

When the plantation system collapsed after the Civil War, these villages grew and joined the existing towns as sites of permanent settlement. Before that war, the Hart Plantation, where Frank grew up, had been owned by the Harts of Hartsville, South Carolina, fame. They quickly left. Charlotte's home had been a part of Bee Hive Plantation, owned by the Bee family. Confederate General Bee was the one who shouted, "There stands Jackson like a stone wall!" They, too, moved on. Left behind on these out-of-the-way places, on these Sea Islands and swamplands, the isolated and self-sufficient Gullah communities continued undisturbed for another century – until malaria was eradicated, air conditioning invented and the Lowcountry was "discovered" by the outside world. Land values soared and a unique way of communal life began to disappear. But still, for Charlotte and Frank's generation, this sense of community remains strong. And related to that sense is the wish of the Gullah descendents to own their own land, a desire often thwarted by high taxes and the complexities of commonly held heirs' property.

OCCUPATIONS

The transition from slavery was strife-ridden and at times brutal, but freed blacks could at least take their professions with them. The majority continued to farm, but usually not under the sharecropping system found elsewhere. Here an individual was more likely to work his own piece of land or work for wages on even larger holdings. Gradually, rice planting was abandoned, first on the large scale and then the small. Both Charlotte's and Frank's parents found rice cheaper to buy than raise. Cotton

was crippled by the arrival of the boll weevil a century ago, and that too was largely abandoned in favor of vegetables – referred to as truck crops. Plowing was done by mule or horse and the hoe continued as a primary implement. A large family meant many hands, and both Charlotte and Frank have clear memories of pulling weeds and picking crops.

Fishing and hunting could also provide a livelihood – and more importantly, a meal. In 1880, Charleston was the nation's leading producer of shrimp and a decade later, little McClellanville, where I live, was the largest producer of terrapin – of turtle soup fame. Weather permitting, a large fleet of sailing bateaus left Charleston each day for the black-fish banks off shore. Remember Porgy in *Porgy and Bess*? He is named after the cheapest of those deep-sea fish. Even Pawleys Island's famed Gray Man was borrowed from these stoic fishermen. To have the Gray Man aboard meant death had come. Oyster canneries, inshore hand-lining and crabbing provided similar opportunities – to both make a living and meet death. And, of course, all this had a tremendous impact on Gullah cooking. With the creek beside you, you would not go hungry. Both Charlotte's and Frank's families understood this well.

The Gullah were our first lumbermen. They worked the great pine forests for what were called ship stores – pine tar, masts and spars, and then harvested the trees for saw mills powered by themselves and by water, wind and steam. I say "themselves" because the first saws were pit saws, one man above, one below, and held between them a long crosscut blade. An early letter describes how the French Huguenot Pierre Manigualt and his slave spent their first six months here working together with just such a contraption. (Note the name and the direct connection to Pierre Manigualt, chairman of today's Evening Post Publishing Company, which has made this book possible.) For centuries, rivers alone were used to float the logs to milling, but by 1900 small logging railroads were winding through the Lowcountry forests, and for the most part these were worked by the Gullah. *"Sleep 'neath the tree"* was often the rule then. You worked and lived beside the track and walked home to your family on weekends. Of course, pines weren't the only trees to be harvested. Cypress swamps were cleared to make rice fields, though most often the trees were burned or buried. In the 1930s, cypress canoes were still a form of transportation for the Gullah, as were split cypress shingles for cabin roofs, which ended in that same decade. By that time, pulp-wooding was the major industry of our woodlands and most of these crews were run and staffed by Gullahs.

Carpenters, brick masons, cattlemen, loggers, butchers and ironworkers were sometimes needed, and many a man could serve as a jack of all trades. I was told that the residents along the Santee collected driftwood that floated by on the river until enough for a house piled up. And there was an efficiency in those early cabin designs that prefabrication companies would do well to study. Cypress shingles kept out the rain. Shutters painted indigo blue kept out the haints. Charlotte's father built their Ten Mile house and Frank's family did the same on Wadmalaw Island. As both Charlotte and Frank point out, a farmer was expected to do it all and maybe preach besides. Women, too, had multiple responsibilities. They nursed children, kept house, tended the garden, sewed, picked crops for larger farmers, and most importantly they cooked for their extended families. Charlotte's mother did all this and worked in a Charleston home, as well. When her grandmother was too old to stand, she hoed while sitting in a chair. "Work" is what Frank remembers of his childhood. Everybody did it all day long.

MEDICINE

With no doctors readily available and no money to pay them when they were, the Gullah population relied most often on folk remedies, primarily herbal cures that had been learned from their African forbearers and the Native American population they met here. Life Everlasting was a tea drunk for practically any purpose, as was brewed sassafras, and for Charlotte and Frank these remedies were so ordinary they hardly bear mentioning. And though fading away, witch doctors were still around – but so was the white medicine man, a self-proclaimed pharmacist who came to the Sea Islands in his station wagon to sell concoctions of fish oil and sulfur. Midwives delivered the babies and a trip to the hospital was rare. You lived or you didn't. God's ways were a mystery.

"Sleep 'neath the tree" was often the rule then. You worked and lived beside the track and walked home to your family on the weekend.

ENTERTAINMENTS

Storytelling was a major form of entertainment and both Charlotte and Frank heard the Br'er Rabbit stories, whose trickster hero relied on his wits to best more powerful opponents – whether fox or bear or the implied plantation master. And ghosts, witches and haints were said to be close by. Store-bought toys were rare. Frank recalls his grandfather's purchase of a Christmas bicycle. Shared by fourteen children and adults, at the end of three months it had been ridden into the ground. Charlotte's first doll baby was made from a certain field grass. Pulled up and washed, the roots were braided into pig tails and two tightly drawn strings defined the head and body. Along with rolling tires and jumping ropes, play was a creative affair. As they grew older, young people danced and picnicked. A church service was entertainment. Meals were entertainments. Family gatherings, barbecues, oyster roasts, weddings and even funerals brought people together – we'll be getting back to those.

THE GULLAH CALENDAR

It's the plague of modernity to view time as a straight line. We start at A and rush to Z. We live our lives cool in summer, warm in winter and, if need be, bright at night and dark during the day. We have lost track of the cyclical experience – the one bred into us by eons of evolution. For the Gullah population, this simply wasn't so. From dawn to dusk is how Charlotte and Frank speak of their young lives, with night used for a short study period and sleep. And at least for their grandparent's generation, the broader passage of time was still a yearly circle. Spring brought rebirth, fields tended, crops planted. Summer brought the ripening of fruit and vegetables, the catching of fish and shrimp. Summertime and the living is easy. It's a lullaby sung by a Gullah nurse. And with fall came activity: harvest, hunting and more fishing, caning and salting, as stores were laid in for winter. And with winter came a period of comparative rest – though there were collards to hoe and oysters to pick, nets to mend and quilts to patch. And all these activities were regulated by the daily hours of sunlight they and the earth beneath them received. The early Catholic Church understood this. They gave us Christmas to celebrate the return of the sun and Easter for further renewal, and we in America have added the celebrations of Thanksgiving and the Fourth of July. For the Gullah these, along with weddings and baptisms, were major events, times when the family came together to give thanks and to dine.

As Charlotte explains, the name for her restaurant came easily enough. She wanted to give the community what she'd received as a child, what for her had been the Gullah experience. It's a restorative and continuing life experience, this eating of meals. As Frank says, Gullah cooking is about "rice" and about kinship. Family and love. Love equals food. Doesn't get much simpler than that.

A GULLAH CUISINE

It's easy enough to romanticize a past state, particularly easy when the ills of this modern age are pressing down. Note that Jonathan Green's Gullah paintings are bright and happy and Mic Smith's thoroughly modern photographs are, as well. In their work, both these artists suggest a strong sense of belonging and a basic joy in living. And in fact, Charlotte remembers her childhood in just those terms. And while Frank might complain that he ate far too many "grits on grits," he feels the same. As Charlotte explains, the name for her restaurant came easily enough. She wanted to give the community what she'd received as a child, what for her had been the Gullah experience. It's a restorative and continuing life experience, this eating of meals. And judging by her customers – blacks, whites and Mexicans – and by the automobiles in the parking lot – twenty-year-old Ford trucks to brand new Mercedes sedans – it is an experience appreciated by all. As Frank says, Gullah cooking is about "rice" and about kinship. Family and love. Love equals food. Doesn't get much simpler than that.

Frank Jenkins:
COMING UP GULLAH

My grandmother and aunts did most of the cooking but all of us could cook something. No refrigerator. No electricity. On a holiday, we'd kill five hogs and use salt to cure them. We'd put the hog in a salt box. Sweet potatoes went in a bank. Sweet potatoes on some pine straw, corn stalk up above like a teepee, with dirt over that. White potatoes we stored in a barn. Shrimp went on the tin roof of the shed to dry out. Instead of ice, we had a tin roof.

I was born on Wadmalaw Island on the third of February 1941 at a place called Hart Plantation. That island is just south of Charleston. I was raised in part by my grandparents. Farming was the big thing. We were on the back side of the island. A creek runs through the area connecting to the Intracoastal Waterway, so coming up we learned early to swim and fish and find our way around in a boat. From six years old on I worked on the farm. Life back then was dark to dark. We went from sunup to sundown. I was raised up with nine boys and four girls, and my grandfather wanted to keep us busy. My grandfather owned his own farm, which was sizable. Very few blacks had them.

Frank Jenkins

My grandmother and aunts did most of the cooking but all of us could cook something. No refrigerator. No electricity. On a holiday, we'd kill five hogs and use salt to cure them. We'd put the hog in a salt box. Sweet potatoes went in a bank – sweet potatoes on some pine straw, corn stalk up above like a teepee, with dirt over that. White potatoes we stored in a barn. Shrimp went on the tin roof of the shed to dry out. Instead of ice, we had a tin roof. We did the same with mullet, dried them on a sheet of tin. We kept the shrimp heads to make a shrimp-based gravy. String beans and other vegetables we'd can, that is, we'd put them in a glass jar. We had apple trees, pear trees – a lot of canning there too.

I remember my grandmother sewing. For the girls, she sewed dresses. In elementary school, we boys wore knickers. We were the only ones, only ones walking around going squeak, squeak. When I got old enough, I went to dungarees. When a person got too old to work on the farm, they'd quilt. A patchwork quilt was all we had to cover with, and there was no heat at night. You could look at the patches and see what everybody had been wearing until they wore those clothes completely out. Either feathers or cotton were used in the mattresses. Chicken feathers were better because they lasted longer. The cotton would ball up. Three or four slept

to a bed. We were crossways on the mattress. The house only had three rooms for sleeping. Girls, boys and my grandparents.

Plain hot irons that you put straight on the stove were replaced with ones that held burning coal on the inside. A big improvement because it stayed hot longer. We didn't buy regular coal or charcoal. We'd cut live oak to make the charcoal that would be used in the iron. We even tried to make some to sell, but couldn't get a big enough quantity. Whatever it took, that's what we did, and it all seems like yesterday.

I started school late. I was almost seven. We had a wood stove in the school and I'd come early and make the fire. I'd get branches from around the building. There was no custodian. We kids did that and the teacher was good to the one who started the fire. We all knew how, but I enjoyed doing it. The teacher was nice to me. We

only had two classes in the elementary. In the early 50s they built a new school in Rockville and we got bused there. The white school had a bus earlier. There were no more than twenty in the white school.

Back then things were a little different. The teacher would crack you on the hand if you didn't do right. I had one who was the meanest little teacher ever. She'd beat you. And you mess with the teacher, you might as well not go home. If they told your mother you were acting up and got beat, you'd get another beating at home. I was a good kid at school.

All the property my great-grandparents acquired after slavery my family still owns. Every inch. And the family bought more. Family was very important. Besides cousins, I had uncles and aunts living on Hart. And most others in the area were family. Everybody I knew could fish and farm. Everybody had those skills – survival skills. We always had abundance to eat. I give a lot of credit to my grandparents. Nine boys, they came out one a lawyer, one a doctor, one an accountant. The rest are businessmen, things of that nature.

When Charlotte and I came back from New York, I wanted to move to Wadmalaw, but the work opportunities were better over by Mount Pleasant. We bought our Ten Mile property from one of Charlotte's cousins. I joined the Mount Pleasant Fire Department and reached the rank of captain. When I retired from that, I started helping Charlotte.

We come from similar backgrounds – cooking backgrounds. In Gullah cooking, we don't waste anything. Here at Gullah Cuisine, if we cook cabbage with ham, we take the ham and chop it up and put it on the mash potatoes with a little cheese on top and we got potato pancakes. You got chicken left over, you make a chicken salad or barbecue chicken. In the Gullah days, people used everything on the pig or cow. Pig feet, hog head. Gullah rice comes from the chicken stewing. Herring rice is the same. Everything you can do with rice the Gullah people did. Coming up, we had neck bone stew – tomato, potatoes, a little salt and pepper, you got neck bone stew. Making do. Family – kin. Being a good neighbor. And tasting right. That's what Gullah cooking is all about.

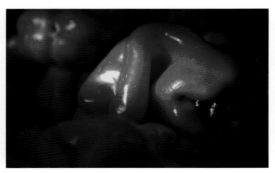

String Bean Harvest, 1994 © Jonathan Green

My grandmother's house was in the pure Gullah tradition. For an inside bathroom, she had a wash bowl on a night stand. There was an old iron bed in the bedroom with a mattress stuffed with chicken feathers, and a homemade quilt. That kitchen of hers just had nails to hang the pots on and a draped cupboard to keep the dishes in. She lived in front of us, just a little cabin, but strongly built. Pecan trees were all around. We'd be in her yard jumping rope or playing Sally Over the Water. That was a game where you join hands and go in a circle singing "Sally over the water, Sally over the sea, Sally catch a black bird, can't catch me." The clothes dryer was in her yard – that was the sun, a clothes line and clothes pins. For a clothes washer, my grandmother had a big black pot. She'd swirl the white clothes in the hot water in the black pot.

- Charlotte

The Wedding, 1988 © Jonathan Green

BAPTISM, MARRIAGE & BURIALS

For slaves, a Christian service depended on memorizing portions of scripture and singing their joyful acceptance of Christ. These expressions are still present in today's Gullah services. Both Charlotte and Frank were brought up in this tradition, and you'll see from their comments how important it was in their lives. The seeking after Christ that they both describe was necessary before a baptism could occur.

These Christian sacraments came early to the Gullah community. Being Christians themselves, most slave owners felt compelled to share their faith with heathen arrivals from Africa – indeed, this conversion was often used as a defense for slavery. Still, those portions of the Bible dealing with the revolt of the Israelite slaves were not to be tolerated. Didn't Pharaoh's army get drowned? This was not an idle question. Special Bibles were printed, ones edited to discourage insurrection, but the safest course was to forbid literacy among the servant class. Submersion in the river goes straight back to John the Baptist. The submersion inside the church is simply a modern version.

Marriage within the slave community was usually encouraged by the plantation owners. Their intent was to both strengthen Christian virtues and increase their slaveholdings. Still, a primary complaint against this "peculiar institution" was that families were frequently broken up by the sale of a husband or wife. It's a happy, if ironic, adaptation that Charlotte's niece would choose Boone Hall Plantation as the site for her "ultimate yard wedding." The plantation house there is a replacement from the 1930s, but close by, beside the oak avenue, are authentic brick slave quarters.

Baptism

Pot Roast or
Baked Chicken

Dirty Rice

Stringbeans

Macaroni & Cheese

Candied Yams

Cornbread

Peach Cobbler

Iced Tea

Jumping the broom was a marriage ceremony of expedience not just in the slave community but all across the Southern frontier. Preachers were often few and far between, and this act of mutual affection was witnessed by the community and hence served until more formal arrangements could be made.

In earlier days, funerals were frequent. Children weren't likely to reach the age of sixteen, a statistic that held true for whites as well. As Charlotte mentions, if an adult died, any infants connected to the family were passed over the grave to free them from the influence of the deceased. Coffins were handmade. Bereavement was open and emotional. Cemeteries were usually on marginal land, but as Frank comments, there were exceptions. The graves seldom had traditional stones and were often decorated with seashells as well as tea cups, clocks and other objects enjoyed in this life. That, too, ended with Frank's and Charlotte's generation.

CHARLOTTE: ON SEEKING

I don't know when seeking ended, but when I was a teenager, probably thirteen or fourteen, I went seeking God. This was what all teenagers wanting to join the church did. Around Easter they had a revival meeting, with singing, shouting, praying. It was called "kneeling at the mourner's bench." You knelt at the altar and prayed and that determined if you were ready to seek.

For four days I just had bread and water and prayed, prayed, prayed. And then I told my dreams to the higher people in the church, those ordained to interpret dreams. Then they decided from those dreams that I was ready. That was it. I came into the church and was baptized. I "join church." The kind of baptism depends on the church, the minister. Some submerge in the water. In our church the minister just anointed the forehead.

> For four days I just had bread and water and prayed, prayed, prayed. And then I told my dreams to the higher people in the church, those ordained to interpret dreams.

Way back when we had church services that lasted all day, people would bring dishes from home and put these out on tables under the trees. They don't do that anymore. Now they have a kitchen attached to the church. Mama was always cooking for the church. She was a favorite with the preachers – not all of them, though. That's how it is in a church.

Back then there was no piano in the church. We just had clapping and singing and shouting. Getting the Holy Ghost, that was the service. For hymns, I remember best: *Down by the River Side. I'm going to lay down my burden down by the river side, down by the river side.* That one always touched me. *Lord I want to be a Christian. Were you there when they nailed Him to the Cross? Swing Low Sweet Chariot. Come Ye Thankful People.* Around Easter we did those revivals and called to the altar,

we'd sing *Blessed Assurance*. A song that leaves you emotional, that's a good song. *Walking to Jerusalem just like John* we sang all the time. We had a gentleman who did a very nice job on *Oh, Mary don't you weep, don't you moan*. When he started it up, everybody rose. I used to sing a lot. I still go to camp meeting some years. The cooking there is on a fire in a big black pot. All your family members get together and spend the night in little houses that are in a circle. Up in the Dorchester area there's a white one everybody knows about. The blacks have one up there, too.

Years ago they used to pass a child over the grave to keep the spirit of the dead from entering him or her. I haven't seen that in years.

As for funeral services: Years ago they used to pass a child over the grave to keep the spirit of dead from entering him or her. I haven't seen that in years. And if you were pregnant, don't look in the coffin because the baby would look like the deceased. In more rural areas they might still do those things. Years ago they'd cover the mirrors in the house. They'd lay the body out on the porch. The whole family would sit up. They stopped that too. There's a funeral home close to Ten Mile. Gravediggers, they're gone as well.

I'm told there's a best-selling book called *The Shack* where the man meets God and God turns out to be a black woman cook who spends all her time cooking good meals for Jesus and the Holy Ghost. Well, I don't know about that. Depends on how you feel, I guess. I always feel like God is within you and whatever it takes … if a black woman cook pleases you, if that's your heaven, that's your heaven.

FRANK: ON SEEKING

When I was nine years old, I went to a gentleman in my church. In order to join the church you had seeking. You had to pray and go through a reading. You'd be instructed by a member. Twice a week you go to him with all your dreams. Me and my brother went. He went to one leader, me another. I'm nine years old and I take the man the dream and he interprets my dream and he tells me if I'm thinking right or wrong. Every night you'd find a spot under an oak tree and pray – in the dark.

You can't do this in the daytime. You're seeking the Lord. You pray. As a kid that's scary. And you couldn't lie and say you went and didn't. The leader could look at you and know you're lying. Some nights I just didn't go. I hoped the Lord would forgive me. I'd go back to him and he'd say, "You missed two nights didn't you?" I'd say, "Yes." He'd say, "Don't miss no more." You tell him the dreams and he sends you back to pray and dream until he thinks you're ready. Six weeks, nine weeks, whatever it takes. He can "read" you and knows if you're ready to go into the church. Sometimes I didn't dream. I'd try to make up a dream and he'd catch me. So I'd try telling the same dream over cause I figure he's an older fellow and won't

remember. He says, "No, you told me that dream last week." "Sir," I said, "I didn't dream nothing." So I go home and go to bed on a full stomach and that helps. One time I dreamt about a girl. I tell him she's a girl in my class and she's hitting me in the head with a pencil and other stuff. He says, "What else you dream about the girl." I couldn't tell him that, but he understood.

Well, he was an oyster shucker. I'd go to him in the afternoon, about four o'clock, just before dark. He'd be shucking the oysters, raw shucking and putting them in jars to sell. After a while, I realize he knows more about me than I know about myself. And he tells me about myself. He has me stand in front of a bunch of ladies and tell them why I'm ready to be accepted as a Christian. And I did. As a kid, you just make up stuff, because you really don't know what's what at nine. They said, "You're ready." Some of the kids, they say, you got to go back. This guy

was the master shucker. He had oyster piles there eight, ten feet high, and it was a one-man operation. He'd go get the oysters and shuck out a couple dozen jars a day. White folks, black folks, they'd come pick the oysters up in the evening.

The old Baptist church was right next to my house, but we went to AME (African Methodist Episcopal). The Baptist only had ten people and it's still that way. AME had sixty-five or seventy people. The old AME church was off the ground and when they clapped and shouted, the church moved. A lively church. It's all in the preacher – whether he can make the people happy. Repetition is an important part. It gets the point across, but sometimes it just meant the speaker didn't know anything else to say. My great-grandfather would get stuck on "and then." It's entertainment and good entertainment at the time. But prayer is how people relate. What's being said in that church is referring to everyday life. "Lord, I know you didn't bring me this far to let me down now." Like that. People are hoping for the best. "Ain't nothing my keenness cost me, but the same lord who brought me this far got me going today." Hope and everyday teaching. Everything that you want to say to the Lord gets said. There's a good sample of this in the book *When Roots Die*. "Lord strengthen us where we are weak, and build us where we are tearing down." My uncle, James Brown, would preach that one.

After I got old enough, I understood that some people leave church and go drinking. They feel like they've done their duty as Christians. I went to church and as a kid I believed in all of it. Growing up, I saw things different. New Year services, they had a countdown. Start singing and praying until the New Year came in. "The watchman is watching the clock. Watchman, what time is it now?" They'd sing. And he'd answer with the time. That would go on right up until midnight. I stopped going because when I was young it was late at night and when I was older I wanted to go to a party. I went to Times Square for the dropping of the ball. I got to tell you, that was better. But I liked church. I went to church because I was afraid of what would happen to me if I didn't go. I was told to go and I believed in Christ just like everybody else. But after I left the island there were other things. On the island the church was the big thing, the only place you could see other people. The island was so remote. And on the farm, you mostly saw family. Prayer meeting was on Thursday night. After you joined the church you had to learn a prayer, a long prayer, but after awhile you all learned to pray. You don't have to say the same thing. You ask for forgiveness, you ask for help. Basically, if you got that in your head you know how to pray. The answering of the congregation, that comes if you're praying and making sense. Then people will cheer you on, and so you get louder and more intense in your praying … and the more you remember of the prayer.

What's being said in that church is referring to everyday life. "Lord, I know you didn't bring me this far to let me down now."

Decorating the graves on Wadmalaw was mostly putting flowers out and surrounding the grave with conch shells if they didn't have the money for a stone. They would put out coffee cups and other personal things. And they'd plant a flower on the spot. They used to bury on the plantations, and these grounds were never owned by the blacks or their churches. In the early 1950s, my great-great-aunt gave the church a piece on the water to use as a graveyard. That always struck me as an unnecessary use of waterfront, but since then I've heard it was the custom. Being on the water made it easier for the dead to fly back to Africa. All my early ancestors are buried on plantation grounds that are overrun by trees or even houses. One woman built her house in the middle of a burial place, but nobody stays there long.

Wedding

Shrimp & Grits

Fried Green Tomatoes

Roast Beef

String Beans

Gullah Rice

Buttermilk Biscuits

Kesha's Sweetgrass Wedding Punch

CHARLOTTE: ON WEDDINGS

We had outside weddings that were called yard weddings. They'd make an arch, a bower out of branches and decorate it. The couple would get under there and the preacher would perform the ceremony. The meal would be something like ham and red rice and a nice salad. For a wedding cake, we had a pound cake. My sister who passed away did the cakes. I used to make them with her, but since she died, I haven't made one. I can remember the recipe in my head: three eggs, three cups of sugar, and the rest. Punch was spiked, moonshine mixed with Julep, a soft drink that came in a bottle from a country store. I don't think they carry it anymore. Flowers came out of the woods.

This was the wedding of my niece, my brother's daughter. She picked Boone Hall Plantation because she'd heard us talking about the weddings of the older people in the family. Her mother and father had a yard wedding. Her first cousin had a wedding in her yard. For the number of people they were inviting, they needed a big yard. Boone Hall was beautiful. So this is a yard wedding. The ultimate yard wedding. I don't know if they had moonshine, but my daughter made a drink called Sweetgrass Punch that went over big.

THE FIRST COWBOYS

The arriving settlers released their cattle into the wilderness to forage and these soon established themselves as semi-wild herds, with the plantation slaves as the herders.

As curious as it sounds, the Gullah were this nation's first cowboys. Historian Peter Wood writes that slaves in the Carolina Lowcountry were referred to as "cowboys" as far back as the seventeenth century. The arriving settlers released their cattle into the wilderness to forage and these soon established themselves as semi-wild herds, with the plantation slaves as the herders. Brands also date back more than three hundred years. The range was open and remained open in much of this area until the 1950s. Often the cattle were simply shot and butchered, but there were roundups and drives, like in the Hollywood movies – the same movies

Frank and his companions imitated with cowboy bull riding.

Both Charlotte and Frank emphasize that in their youth beef cattle were for selling not consumption. Of course, they serve beef today, and sometimes it comes from the most thoroughbred of cattle. Charlotte is good friends with an Awendaw cattlewoman, whose handsome livestock is pictured here. As in olden times, the fences extend into the marsh and the live oaks are eternal.

FRANK:
COWS ON THE FARM

We had three bulls – Jimmy, Pete and Blackie. Me and my uncles would take them out where the honeysuckle was high and thick so they couldn't buck much, and ride them. Then once we had them tired we'd take them in the plowed field and really ride them – like cowboys, like the real bull riders. One bull was part Brama – that's the hardest I've ever been thrown by anything in my life. You go up in the air, he slaps you down. That was the first time I was ever knocked out. This is our entertainment I'm describing. My grandfather said they were poor creatures that had no way to defend themselves, so we did it behind his back.

On our farm I don't remember but one beef cow being slaughtered. They were raised for money and went to the market in Walterboro. We usually had three cows for milk. The milk wasn't pasteurized. In the icebox (the kind with just ice) it would last four or five days. The cream came to the top – three inches thick on top. The butter I never liked. Too milky. Grandmama and my aunts would churn it. To make homemade ice cream, the same churning theory applied. Some of the milking cows were tied out in the field. We'd also treat them to hay and corn, so they'd give more. We'd bring them to the shed to milk. My uncle, the one who became a doctor, was good at this. It took me two hands, pulling and pressing at the same time to keep the cow steady. Wang, wang, wang. And you have a bucket of milk. You let the calf suck first to calm the cow.

The cow in this photograph is a modern Awendaw cow. Mrs. Sue Drew has a ranch up there in Awendaw where she breeds cattle to sell. These are special cows. Very expensive. Back on Wadmalaw Island we had plain cows. Until I took agriculture classes in high school, I didn't know there was any other kind.

The Congregation, 1990 © Jonathan Green

THE CHRISTIAN HOLIDAYS

The Gullah tradition of Hoppin' John and collards at New Year's goes with the saying, "Eat poor that day, eat rich the rest of the year."

Linked to the spread of Christianity among the Gullah was the celebration of the holidays. Thanksgiving, Christmas, New Year's and Easter were in slavery days a time of at least limited rest, moments of plenty and joyous celebration. The day was usually set aside from labor and an extra ration was provided. As children, Charlotte and Frank experienced these holidays most often through the church. Not surprising, except in the case of New Year's which was accomplished in a darkened church with "watchmen" shouting out the hour, some churches even had nativities where the cattle and donkeys spoke and bowed down to the Christ child. Forgive Frank for claiming he enjoyed Times Square more. The Gullah tradition of Hoppin' John and collards at New Year's goes with the saying, "Eat poor that day, eat rich the rest of the year." Of course, holiday menus played a big part and that's what we've included. Around these tables, families, friends and neighbors gather. The best of tableware is brought out. Flowers are arranged, songs sung, laughter heard, stories told. Children have free rein – within reason. And dinner is served.

Easter

Roast Lamb

Lemon Rice

Sweet Potato Fritters

String Beans

Black Beans

Macaroni & Cheese

Corn Muffins

Peach Cobbler

New Year's

Roasted Pork

Okra Pilau

Barbecue Pigs' Feet

Collard Greens

Hoppin' John or Peas & Rice

Corn Muffins

Bread Pudding

CHARLOTTE: ON CHRISTMAS AND NEW YEAR'S

When I was growing up with all those children in the house, there wasn't much money for presents. But we always had something. For Christmas trees we'd go in the woods and cut one down. The decorations came from the same place – moss, red berries and popcorn berries. The popcorn berries are also called tallow berries. We'd string them and drape the moss. Now, my Christmas tree stays up a long time. My grandbaby wanted a tree. We haven't had time to take it down. I said, "Frank take it down." He said, "I didn't put it up. It's fresh cut and a little of the aroma is still in the house. We'll keep it up a while longer." These photographs give a pretty good picture of our Christmas. Lots of singing and happiness, Frank deep frying a turkey. A lot of family.

For New Year's we cook field peas for good luck. You eat them with collards, the greens being for the money and peas for the luck. We have that at New Year's with roasted pork. No spinach. It's got to be collards.

Thanksgiving

Fried Turkey

Seafood Casserole

Gullah Rice

Herring Pilau

Collard Greens

String Beans

Macaroni & Cheese

Candied Sweet Potatoes

Buttermilk Buscuits

Bread Pudding with Hard Sauce

Apple Pie

Christmas
Stuffed Pork Chops

Roasted Turkey

Dirty Rice

Oyster Pilau

Rutabaga

Succotash

Pinto Bean Pie

Sweet Potato Soufflé

Okra Soup

Hoe Cake

Pecan Pie

Apple Pie

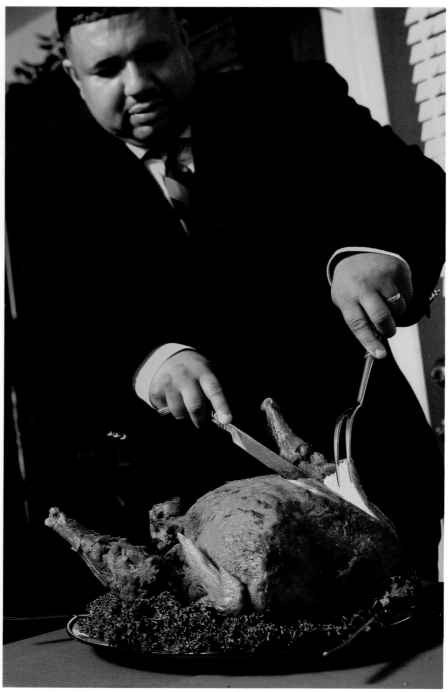

Red Brick Greyhounds, 1988 © Jonathan Green

FUN AND GAMES

Children's games and entertainments. Surely you can judge the health of a culture by the ability of the children to play. Despite their exacting work schedules, young Charlotte and Frank found time for play. And in the best of the Gullah tradition, this meant finding pleasure in the simplest of material possessions.

FRANK:
ON LIVING & PLAYING
AT THE WATER'S EDGE

For toys and recreation, we didn't have much. One Christmas my grandfather bought one bicycle. It lasted about three months. We kids rode it three at a time. Even the adults rode it. We rode it into the ground. We did have a homemade wheelbarrow to play with and that held up better. Checker playing we did with a homemade board and soft drink caps. Caps up and caps down were the two sides. No baseball – not regular baseball, anyway. We'd make up a baseball game with a stick of wood for a bat. And we had a truck tire. When we were real young, we'd roll in the tire. There are lots of things you can do with a tire. We had a tire hanging by a rope from a tree limb over the water. If you didn't know how to swim, the older ones would throw you out the boat. That worked. You learned to swim fast. I played football in high school and was pretty good. I had a scholarship to play in college but didn't stay with that.

Mosquitoes and gnats were bad in the summer time. But as a child it didn't matter. A lot of gnats just meant good fishing and shrimping. We'd fan them away or run from them. One cousin had a nickname of "Finny Gator." A finny gator is

a fascinating bug, a tumble-top bug. He played with them so much we called him Finny Gator. And we had the doodle bugs – those ant lions that wait at the bottom of a little sand pit. We had lightening bugs in the summer. I couldn't wait to play with them, to put them in a jar and watch. They say the pesticides have killed them. Maybe. I haven't seen them in years.

When I was a seeker, the old man I had to talk to picked oysters and I went with him one time. He'd get a boatload and come in, dump that and go for a second trip on the same tide. He just wore regular boots and walked the bank. The boat was as close in as possible. He'd cull the oysters on the bank and throw them into the boat. Sometimes he carried them over with a half-bushel basket or a bucket.

We didn't get nylon nets until the sixties. The net makers used cotton. A section of cow horn was used to run the tie strings through. The weights were any kind of round lead. They made them, too. A nylon net doesn't sink as fast. Once the cotton is wet it's heavier, and sinks faster and you catch more shrimp. But it's

harder to spread than the nylon.

Charleston's Mosquito Fleet is famous. Men went off shore in sailing bateaus to catch black fish. And I do remember a place called Mosquito Beach that might be connected. On the way over to Folly Beach was this boat landing with some old buildings. My friends the Bachmans packed seafood nearby, so these had probably been fish houses. By the time I came along they were juke joints, four or five of them right on the water. I was thirteen when I went there. They wouldn't let us in, so we went 'round the back where there was a boat and used that to circle in front. I got to watch B.B. King. James Brown came there, too. That was Mosquito Beach. When I was up in New York, I went to all the jazz clubs. I loved jazz and still have lots of albums. Charlotte caters for the festival at Chuma Gallery, which is where this photograph was taken. But back in the young age, it was mostly work. Work never ended. There was always something to do, even if it was to pull grass out of the field.

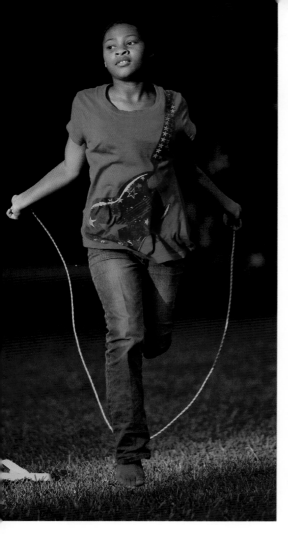

Coming up, we'd make grass dolls. We'd pull the grass up. The fine roots we'd wash and bleach 'til they were white and then we'd braid those to make the hair.

CHARLOTTE:
ON LIVING & PLAYING AT TEN MILE

In the beginning, we had no electricity. We had a hand pump in the yard. Mama cooked on a wood stove. Coming up, my brothers had fire duty. They chopped the wood and always had the wood box full. In the mornings, they'd catch the fire, get things warmed up. Then I'd come and start breakfast, or my mama would. The stove is still there in her house.

Mama put flowers on the table from out of the yard. Every year little yellow lilies would pop up. We'd pick those and put them on the table, those and the little sunflowers, the swamp daisies. When you pick them, they have a funny smell. She didn't grow zinnias or the rest. We did have four o'clocks – the blossoms opened in late afternoon and closed by morning. We had one large shrub with a banana-like leaf. I'm not sure of the name. There were different flower names in different communities. Mint and catnip grew right outside the door. The flower beds and walkway were lined with conchs, and oyster shell was laid down for the walk. Mama swept the yard with a broom. No lawn. Maybe that was to keep the snakes and mosquitoes away. No space was wasted. Potatoes grew in the front yard. The chicken pen was behind the house and the hog pen behind that. We had a peach tree, an apple tree, a pear tree and one pecan tree that's still there right out front. The old hand pump is still there, too, but minus a handle.

Ten Mile was my neighborhood. We have Six Mile, Twelve Mile and Fifteen Mile communities and some others. They were named after how many miles from Charleston the stage coach had traveled. Each place had its own identity, own people, own church. You might not think Six Mile and Ten Mile are far apart. Well, when you have to walk, you'll see "four miles" that way. And we walked a lot of the time. The first school I went to was in the big yellow house that is still on the highway in Ten Mile. A little one-room building in the yard was the first grade. I was very shy. I wouldn't eat in front of the other students. I went there up to third grade, then went to Jennie Moore Elementary and from there to Lang High. School was fun. Home Economics was my best subject. I learned to sew and made a couple of aprons. I already knew how to cook. I was in school with Mary Jackson, who is now the famous sweetgrass basket sewer. Last year she won a half-million-dollar MacArthur grant. It's called a "Genius Grant," and I'm proud to say that I looked at her baskets many years ago and said, "Mary, you're a genius." I never learned basket making myself. It was a Six Mile thing. Not something girls from Ten Mile did. Remember, Six Mile is a different place. Maybe I'll retire some day and learn to sew a basket.

Coming up, we'd make grass dolls. We'd pull the grass up. The fine roots we'd

wash and bleach 'til they were white and then we'd braid those to make the hair. We'd cut bangs across the front, then tie a string at the top of the grass to make the head and at the bottom to make the body, and braid the roots. Those were our doll babies, our "white" doll babies. I don't know if I could even spot that grass now. My grandmama lived in McClellanville. In the summer she'd come spend a week, and she'd do my hair. She'd take a white string with knots in it, wrap braids around that, and leave it in my hair until school started. Oh, I hated that. When I got to be a teenager, I said no more.

Girls had jump roping and hopscotch. We'd mark the bare ground and hop one-legged back and forth. We had the double-Dutch, two ropes going and you jump between them. We'd sing, "Jump little Susie, jump, jump jump. Jump, jump jump 'til you jump overboard." It's a different world now. In some ways the other one was much better. Later we had store-bought dolls. My aunt from the city bought me a real doll and a doll house. She's the one who named me. I was her godchild. She named me Charlotte after herself. They called me Little Charlotte.

Ten Mile wasn't as isolated as the Sea Islands. People had cars instead of mules and wagons. They didn't grind sugar cane or grow much rice. Here people got television. Everything got modernized. I was 14 when we got a television. Our family was the first and we'd charge a nickel to watch TV. My father would take the cord and hide it so we wouldn't watch. He made us do our homework first.

ONE- AND TWO-POT MEALS

Gullah cooking is distinguished by its simplicity, a virtue of necessity that was refined into a cuisine.

For the slaves, one-pot cooking, the pilaus and gumbos were brought with them from their African cooking fires. The word *pilau* – which can be spelled many ways: *perlau, perleau, perlo, purloo* are just a few – can be traced through the French Huguenot settlers back to Persia. Rice had been grown in Africa for thousands of years and needed no introduction, but the seasonings and variety of preparations is a Gullah contribution. One- and two-pot creations found their way from the campfires and slave cabin fireplaces into the kitchens of the owners – and with the end of slavery, into the cookbooks of the owners. We forget these were once open-fire recipes, that heat and smokiness were to be skillfully manipulated. Several of Charlotte's one-pot recipes are listed, but we've also included Frank's more modern canned versions, his two-pot pulpwood crew open-fire Gullah treats. Campers pay attention.

Charlotte's Ascue grandfather was a pulp-wooder who came down from North Carolina and Frank's grandfather ran a successful timber business. As you'll see, Frank preferred this to farming and spent his teenage summers in the pine woods. Like most everything else in the world, the harvesting of pulpwood is now a highly mechanized corporate endeavor.

FRANK:
ON PULP-WOODING,
FARMING AND TWO-POT MEALS

My older uncles did the pulpwood and the younger boys worked on the farm. I preferred the pulpwood, in part, 'cause I liked getting away from home. To cut pulpwood, we'd go in different areas besides Wadmalaw – Hollywood, James Island, further. And as we were in the woods and not many stores around, we did our own cooking. Two logs with a fire between, a frying pan, a deep skillet to do the vegetable and meat and a second skillet to do the rice. Every meal, the same amount of rice. Seven guys working, my uncles with a couple of hired laborers. My job was to cut the limbs off once the tree was down. I did this until ten o'clock. Then I'd go to the staging area and start cooking.

Four basic meals we cooked: tomato-based fish and rice with Lucks beans out the can. Next day would be corned beef out the can. For that, we'd fry the bacon first and get the bacon grease, then add the rice. Next day would be corned beef hash, that and rice and vegetable. Every day was rice and vegetable. Last day would be stew beef, sometimes that out the can too. Occasionally we did have fried fish or fried chicken, but that took time and we usually stuck with food that was quick, what we could cook in an hour. My uncle taught me most of this. I had some uncles younger than me. He was an older uncle.

Cooking outside like that on a wood fire took some skill. You burn the wood down while you're cooking the rice. By the time the wood becomes coals, the rice is boiled. You finish it on the coals. There's space there for two pans, for bacon and the rest. And maybe a small pot on the side for the beans. Sometimes I did this during school – didn't make it to school every day. I'd go to work instead. I spent the summertime in the woods.

We had a horse to ride. That was transportation for my grandfather and that got us to the store, which was a mile and five-eights away.

The pulpwood was the short logs, seven-foot sticks that could be loaded onto a truck by one man, maybe two. Nowadays, they put the whole log on with a machine. Sometimes we'd be following loggers and putting the smaller part of the log on our truck, but usually we'd make a staging area and use the tractor to pull the logs in. At first we used horses or mules for this, and crosscut saws to bring the trees down. Then at the staging area we used another crosscut to cut into length. Crosscut, that's man powered. I've still got a one-man crosscut saw at the house. Gas chainsaws came along in the late fifties. Those were heavy. We used them to bring the tree down. Then at the staging area we had a gasoline saw with a circular blade on wheels – roll and cut. Finally we got out of the pulpwood business. And

not long after I went up to New York.

We had a horse to ride. That was transportation for my grandfather and that got us to the store, which was a mile and five-eights away. I plowed with a mule and a horse. My great-grandfather lived on a place called Tacky Point, a mile or so from Hart Plantation. We'd go help him plow when we finished with our own work. We used trace trains and a single tree. Two trace trains to the horse and a bridle to keep him straight. A hang went over the horse's shoulder so he can pull from the shoulder. I was ten, eleven, twelve when I was plowing.

My family still farms today in the same area. My uncles are still on Wadmalaw. We did big farming. Most of the blacks in that area had to work for white farmers. We in the family had enough to pick of our own and didn't work for the white farmers. Beets, carrots, potatoes, we sold at the market in Charleston and also at the market on Johns Island – called "The Shed." We did keep some to eat, but we planted to sell. Turnips, collards, beets and carrots went to the market. Potatoes and the bigger bulk items, truckers would come and buy. You got twenty boxes of potatoes, somebody else have twenty and the truck come and take them to the market. Cotton we didn't mess with. We planted rice at one time, but it was cheaper to buy. Rice isn't the easiest crop to harvest. We put it in a low area and in order to plow there you had to wait for a dry spell. Then you had to cover the plants with water. I don't think it tasted as good as the processed rice. We ground the rice when I was much younger and ate a lot of it. I know the difference.

My grandfather always had the farm and the pulpwood, and he made a good living. We had mules and horses but we were the earliest farmers on the island to have tractors and trucks. We'd do a big crop of watermelons and take them off in a truck to sell. Those sales on Johns Island and around would buy our school clothes. We didn't get paid for working on the farm, so that was our pay and a lot of fun besides because we'd see a lot of people … and we'd get the girls selling those watermelons. Fun plus we made money. And we'd give a few away. My grandfather believed in helping people. All the people who lived near us could go in the field and help themselves to the crop regardless of whether you invited them or not. My grandfather felt like if you were that hungry, then take something.

My grandfather believed in helping people. All the people who lived near us could go in the field and help themselves to the crop regardless of whether you invited them or not.

Tiger Farm Bus, 1994 © Jonathan Green

Time to Rejoice, 2005 © Jonathan Green

LANGUAGE AND THE ORAL TRADITION

The Gullah language is a time machine. Both Charlotte and Frank understand the value of preserving this poetic cultural tradition, but both also understand the importance of proper English for communicating and hence making a living in the modern world.

Saying *axe* for ask is a quaint remnant of Elizabethan English, one traceable to the Scot and Irish overseers who were the slaves' earliest English instructors. The Gullah language is a time machine. Both Charlotte and Frank understand the value of preserving this poetic cultural tradition, but both also understand the importance of proper English for communicating and hence making a living in the modern world.

Charlotte and Frank grew up in an oral tradition, what's known in the non-academic world as storytelling. Superstitions, ghost stories and tall tales were standard fare as children. Already being children of a modern age, neither claims to have been particularly impressed. Both laughingly declare it was a way for the oldest to instruct the youngest in proper behavior – to frightening them if necessary. Their own grandchildren have turned to books.

FRANK:
ON TALKING GULLAH

How you spoke, how you lived. That was Gullah. My uncle was up in Michigan. He met Patricia Jones-Jackson, a woman scholar up there, and told her about Wadmalaw Island. She came down and lived with the people and wrote the book *When Roots Die: Endangered Traditions of the Sea Islands*. She lived it, saw it, or heard it and didn't lie about nothing. My family members were interviewed for that book. Another of my uncles has a whole long prayer in there. There are only about five hundred in the black community, maybe less now, and she got a good sampling.

She planned to write more but was killed in an auto accident.

Until the age of four, I was living in Baltimore. The first thing I heard when I got to school on Wadmalaw was: *Who pa you from?* I had a real education coming. *Hunna. Who hunna is?* That's who are you? Of course, *ya'll* is more than one. A *biddy* is a small chicken. A *buckra* is a white man. My grandfather used the term but not in later years.

Speaking Gullah – it seemed natural. You get up to New York and you're hearing a hundred foreign languages, and I attended high school there for a short time. I had to learn English just like any immigrant. In fact, some of the foreigners had more standard English than I did. It didn't matter what course I took – math and history, any of it, I had to struggle. To write a paper, I had to go in the dictionary. Now it works the other way. If I go further south, down below Wadmalaw Island, I can't understand the really old Gullah speakers, especially when they get excited and talk fast.

Some of it's not so bad. *Out the light.* That's turn it off. *This side* means Wadmalaw Island. *Pull off my hat* means get out of here. *Day clean.* That's the sun is shining. *One day among all. One day above the rest.* That's trickier. *Nothing for sweet mouth. And long eye.* I remember those particularly 'cause they had to do with girls. Using *e* or *he* instead of he and she was common. I was in Charleston the other day and heard this: *You out here acting up. I gonna tell your aunt on you.* She says, *How you going tell she on me, and me and she the same old.* She was saying her aunt is her age.

I remember the storytellers on the island. Mr. Ted Williams had the first black store on Martin Point. That old gentleman told fairy tales, stories to frighten kids or instruct them. And the tradition is still around. My daughter won a scholarship telling one. I heard Br'er Rabbit, Br'er Wolf, Br'er Gator. But those stories didn't interest me because I knew they were false. I never liked the fake even as a child. I don't watch movies. As I mentioned, my mother started raising me in Baltimore. I barely remember Baltimore. I was four when I came to Wadmalaw. I'd never heard those stories until then. When I did, I didn't believe them.

CHARLOTTE : ON STORYTELLING

Ghost stories. My uncle used to tell them. Where my father used to plant there was a big oak tree and we were told an eight-foot lady lived under that tree. At night, we'd run into her. The one that really sticks with me is about a little girl who

picked a fig. It is too gruesome to repeat. Mind your parents was the moral. And we had to watch out for the hags. When I was a little girl there was a man accused of being a hag. Actually there were several people called hags. They were older people. Looking back, I can see they each had little funny ways. I guess that's why they were called hags. To catch a hag, you watch where he walked and you stick a brand new needle in his tracks. He or she would not be able to go further. They would keep turning around and around. For awhile they couldn't get where they were going. They'd be in a daze. And salt and pepper worked. You find where the hag has left his skin and you salt it. He can't get back in his skin.

Witch doctors. There was one in Awendaw, but he's dead. Some of the people around Ten Mile would go to Beaufort and see Dr. Buzzard. He was famous for his roots and spells. It's the believers who drove all that way. For a real doctor, my grandmama went to Dr. Durst. As children we were carried to Roper Hospital, to the clinic. Now they're building a Roper branch nearly in Ten Mile.

Some of the people around Ten Mile would go to Beaufort and see Dr. Buzzard. He was famous for his roots and spells.

The Bottle Tree, 2003 © Jonathan Green

REMEDIES AND MEDICINE

It was common for early cookbooks to have home remedies listed in the appendixes. With doctors few and far between, the Colonial wife was expected to tend both her family and her servants – and in the South, these cures were often borrowed from the slaves, who had often borrowed from Native Americans. As the children of Gullah parents, Charlotte and Frank were both treated with home remedies.

CHARLOTTE:
ON CURES

Herb cures are a part of the Gullah tradition. They were such a normal part of my growing up I don't even think about them as being different. If we were to step on a nail – there was always stuff in the yard – Mama would take a piece of butts meat, a piece of salt pork, and put it on the nail hole and tie it tight. We'd wear that for awhile. That was supposed to draw all the poison out of the wound. None of us got tetanus, so it did work. Take the spider web and put it on a cut to stop the bleeding. We'd get a cold, she'd brew Life Everlasting Tea. At one point, they banned that because they thought it contained something harmful, but people still boil the leaves and add lemon for a cold cure. Some put a little liquor in there, moonshine or whatever. That made you sweat at night. Sassafras tea was for upset stomach. Pine gum was for boils. Elderberry made a wine. Wild cherry bark made a tea for colds. So did garlic.

FRANK:
ON FOLK REMEDIES

Miss Josephine. She was the midwife. She delivered everybody including me. They took me to the he hospital three days later to be registered. My Uncle Ed is younger than me. I remember him being born, Miss Josephine coming to the house, and the crying baby. For medicines, we had all the usual cures. For a cold, my grandfather brewed up Life Everlasting, which I think is dog fennel. He made it by the quart. Rock candy, olive oil, corn liquor and Life Everlasting. You take a shot and you sweat all night. It sweats the cold out of you. Trust me. The medicine man came by in a station wagon. In the forties and fifties, he'd drive up in the yard with all types of medicine in the car. He'd be on Wadmalaw on Tuesday, then

Quilts in the Wind, 2007 © Jonathan Green

John's Island on Wednesday. For colds, he sold a thick, white fish oil product called Scourge of Merchantine. It did okay but my grandfather's cure did better – that cure of olive oil, moonshine and Life Everlasting. Combine all those ingredients, you had to get better. The Life Everlasting by itself worked if you boiled it long enough and made a strong tea. I think they outlawed that now.

For an infection, my grandfather tied fat back on the cut. Just wrap the butts meat on. And it did work. I don't know why. To stop bleeding they'd just tie the wound tight. People used to use cobwebs, and some put flour on a bleeding wound. That would stop the flow, but how do you wash it off? Necessity was the rule. You didn't go to a doctor, or the hospital. I went to Roper Hospital in elementary school because I was hit by a thrown baseball bat, which was just a sharp piece of wood. I had a hole in my leg. The teacher took me home instead of to a doctor. I stayed home until my grandfather was taking a pulpwood load to North Charleston and he dropped me off at Roper Hospital, which they said was good or I'd have gotten gangrene and lost the leg. That's how things worked back then. Lucky we had a truck or I'd be one-legged. Snake root we'd dig up for a tea but I don't think it worked. Sassafras or *satisfact* tea was used for colds, but the truth is any kind of root you had they would say was a cure for anything. Sassafras tasted good. Who knows if it worked?

Witch doctors were around, but I don't remember any being on Wadmalaw Island. People would go all the way to Beaufort to see Dr. Buzzard. Dr. Buzzard's trick was to psychoanalyze you. You'd talk to him about your problem and in the end he could tell you things about yourself that you didn't think he could possibly know. Then he'd ask if somebody has done you particular harm, somebody trying to poison you, whatever. Then he tells you how to protect yourself. And if you want to put the root on somebody, he's got the little root there and gives instruction. When I say "you" I don't mean "me." Even when I was young I didn't see how anybody could harm me that way … unless they poisoned my food or something. To put some dust around my yard would do nothing, and I knew that for a fact. My family never spoke of roots. But when I was coming up some people in other areas of Wadmalaw would say, "My mama going to put the root on you." I'd say, "Okay, I got me some root too." All I could figure was they had the root of a sassafras or some other funny looking root. They'd dry it out, put in a bag and that's where the name came from. And if you believe they can harm you, then it is scary. When I came to Ten Mile they had a guy up in Fifteen Mile called the Root Man. He had these chicken feathers hanging up and a chicken foot hanging up – a real witch doctor. Some say this magic came from Africa. And if you believe in it they can get your money. But that man was the last I heard of, and he died.

Decoration Day, 1992 © Jonathan Green

THE FOURTH OF JULY

Following the loss of the Civil War, white Carolinians usually chose to ignore Independence Day. The freed Gullah felt just the opposite, and the Fourth was their holiday, one marked by picnics and excursions.

The Fourth of July is our great national holiday, one referenced by pledges of allegiance to the flag, fried chicken, watermelon and fireworks displays. But here in the Lowcountry it wasn't always so. Following the loss of the Civil War, white Carolinians usually chose to ignore Independence Day. They considered themselves to be a conquered province and there was nothing to be gained by celebrating the conqueror, especially here where the first shot of that lost war was fired. Needless to say, the freed Gullah felt just the opposite and the Fourth was their holiday, one marked by picnics and excursions. Returning from the First World War, Southern troops refused to march beside the Yankee divisions for the

New York victory parade, but at least they had fought and the notion of a United States was again taking hold. World War II completed this transition and now it's red, white and blue flags and fried chicken for everybody. And being ever-generous, the Gullah people are happy to share.

CHARLOTTE:
ON PICNICS & INDEPENDENCE DAY

For beach parties, we'd go to Atlantic Beach where the black folks go. We didn't swim. They had a juke box. We'd go there and get all the latest dances. That's when I was teenager. A picnic lunch was baloney sandwiches and deviled eggs. At the end of Gadsenville Road where the marsh and creek started, we had a ball field. The ball games were a celebration. And where Beehive Road came to the marsh we had a pavilion that stuck out and caught the sea breeze. We'd dance there. They had a swing that swung out over the marsh. This really was like those Jonathan Green paintings. The ball field has been moved and the pavilion is now just a short post in the marsh.

These days we celebrate the Fourth at one another's house. These photographs were taken at my brother's.

Sunday Dinner, 1997 © Jonathan Green

FRANK:
GRANDDADDY'S
SUNDAY BREAKFAST

My grandmother worked in the field but still did most of the cooking. My aunts did some. They were excellent cooks and there was always plenty on the table. They used a wood stove and an icebox. That was Gullah cooking, that's safe to say. Fresh and canned vegetables, fresh seafood, pork, corn and rice. Chickens and fresh eggs. Venison. Fresh milk from our own cows. We had all that. And everybody in the family could cook bread, even the boys.

We had three meals a day: breakfast, dinner, supper. Dinner was the big meal. We had corn bread – fried bread – in the morning. Fried bread means it's not a pancake. Bread made of water and flour, not much in it. Dinner we'd have after school. Supper was light. We only had a couple of hours to do homework. Then go to sleep. At night we had bread and milk. Bread and syrup. Bread and bread. Every night was bread.

My grandfather would cook on Sunday morning. He was a very religious fellow but didn't go to church until his later days. He'd do biscuits. He did a mean biscuit. But don't ask if he was a better biscuit maker than Charlotte. I can't say. When I was a boy, his biscuits tasted mighty good and now I don't eat biscuits. Maybe I ate too many when I was a kid. Biscuits and grits I don't eat. Grits on grits. I have to confess – I hate grits. But as a boy I liked them well enough.

Those Sunday breakfasts of my grandfather's do stick in my mind. Biscuits from scratch. Salted pork in a gray gravy of onions and flour. Grits, of course. Sometimes fried fish or stewed. This was mullet or whiting. Shrimp and grits. That recipe and the one for the pork is the same that Charlotte gives. Coffee to drink.

Sunday was the only morning we had a sit down to breakfast. The rest of the time we'd be going off to work or school and just grabbed something on the way. Sunday we sat down with the family. Sunday was the day of rest and then we were off to Sunday School and church. My grandfather created something for us children. "An idle mind is a wasted mind," is what he said. I was a grandchild and most of the rest were his own children, but he didn't show favoritism. If you were smart and did the work, he complimented you. If not, he gave you hell. A straightforward, no-nonsense fellow who cooked a mean biscuit and made us Sunday breakfast.

Frank's Granddaddy's Sunday Breakfast

Biscuits

Pork & gravy

Fried or stewed fish (Mullet or whiting)

Shrimp and grits

Coffee

Red Tomatoes, 1992 © Jonathan Green

Chapter Three
THE RECIPES

Farm Animals, 1993 © Jonathan Green

From our Garden, 1991 © Jonathan Green

Gullah
BASICS

Gullah Seasoning

Gullah Seasoning for Baking and Roasting

Gullah Seasoning for Fried Foods

Gullah Barbecue Rub

Gullah Barbecue Sauce

Gullah Seafood Seasoning

Fish Stock

Chicken Stock

Brown Stock

White Sauce

Gullah Seafood Seasoning

An all-purpose seasoning for baking, stews, grilling and frying

Combine all ingredients. Store in a tightly closed container. Will keep for 3 months in a dark cool place, or in the freezer for up to a year.

1/4 cup granulated garlic

1/4 cup granulated onion

1/4 cup salt

1/4 cup black pepper

1/4 cup celery salt

1 tablespoon + 1 teaspoon ground dry mustard

1 tablespoon + 1 teaspoon paprika

2 teaspoons ground bay leaf

2 teaspoons red pepper flakes

2 teaspoons ground ginger

2 teaspoons ground allspice

2 teaspoons ground cardamom

1 teaspoon ground cloves

1 teaspoon ground mace

1 1/2 pounds fish bones and heads (grouper or flounder recommended)

2 gallons water

3 ribs celery, chopped in large pieces

2 large onions (about 1 pound), peeled and chopped in large pieces

2 bay leaves

1/4 teaspoon dried thyme leaves

1/4 teaspoon black peppercorns

1 sprig parsley

Fish Stock

Makes 6 1/2 quarts

Juice from a fish head is perfect for flavoring. French cooking depends on it. But when I was a child we were stewing fish heads and my mama didn't get that out of a French cookbook. That was our stock, what we made gravy from. The fishermen would come by the house and sell their fresh-caught fish.

-**Charlotte**

Place the fish bones and heads, water, celery and onion in a stockpot. Tie the bay leaves, thyme, peppercorns and parsley up in cheesecloth and add. Briskly simmer uncovered for 2 1/2 hours, skimming off any foam that rises.

Strain and use immediately or cool to room temperature cover and refrigerate. Tightly covered, fish stock will keep for up to 2 days in the refrigerator or up to 3 months in the freezer.

Chicken Stock

Makes 1 gallon

Rinse the chicken bones to remove any excess blood. Place the chicken bones, water, celery, carrots and onion in a stockpot. Tie the bay leaves, thyme, peppercorns and parsley stems in cheesecloth and add. Briskly simmer uncovered for 3 hours, skimming off any foam. Strain and use immediately or cool to room temperature, cover and refrigerate.

Tightly covered, chicken stock will keep for up to 2 days in the refrigerator or up to 3 months in the freezer.

3 pounds chicken bones (backs & necks)

1 1/2 gallons water

3 ribs celery, chopped in large pieces

3 carrots, peeled and chopped in large pieces

2 large onions (about 1 pound), peeled and chopped in large pieces

2 bay leaves

1/4 teaspoon dried thyme leaves

1/4 teaspoon black peppercorns

3 parsley stems

4 pounds beef bones, preferably with some meat still on them

2 gallons water

3 ribs celery, chopped in large pieces

3 carrots, peeled and chopped in large pieces

2 large onions (about 1 pound), peeled and chopped in large pieces

3 bay leaves

1/4 teaspoon dried thyme leaves

1/4 teaspoon black peppercorns

3 parsley stems

Brown Stock

Makes 5 quarts

Preheat oven to 400 degrees. Place the beef bones in a roaster. Add the celery, carrots and onions and roast them uncovered for approximately 3 hours, until they brown, turning them over occasionally to brown them on all sides and to prevent burning.

Remove the bones and vegetables from the roaster and put them in a stockpot. Add 1/2 cup of the water to the drippings in the roaster. Scrape up all of the brown drippings from roaster and add them and the remaining water to stockpot. Tie the bay leaves, thyme, peppercorns and parsley up in cheesecloth and add. Briskly simmer uncovered for 3 hours, skimming off any foam that rises. Strain and use immediately or cool to room temperature, cover and refrigerate.

Tightly covered, beef stock will keep for up to 2 days in the refrigerator or up to 3 months in the freezer.

White Sauce

Makes 4 cups

A white sauce is made with milk. We had a cow that I was too young to milk. My older sister did that. With all that cream on the top, I remember it as being the best milk. The white sauce goes into casseroles and cream soups.

-**Charlotte**

Melt the butter in a heavy-bottomed pot. Whisk in the flour. Cook for 2 minutes, whisking gently. Slowly whisk in the milk, being sure to whisk out any lumps. Cook, whisking occasionally, for about 10 minutes, or until the sauce is thick enough to coat the back of a spoon. Add the mace, salt and white pepper.

Use immediately or cool, cover and refrigerate for up to 2 days.

4 ounces unsalted butter

1/4 cup self-rising flour

4 cups milk

1/4 teaspoon mace

1/4 teaspoon salt

1/4 teaspoon white pepper

Green Tomatoes, 1994 © Jonathan Green

Gullah
APPETIZERS

Kesha's Boiled Peanuts

Sweet Potato Fritters

Crispy Conch Fritters

Crab Balls

Fried Green Tomatoes

Black-Eyed Pea Dip

Lowcountry Shrimp Boil – "Gullah Style"

Lowcountry Shrimp Boil – "Gullah Style"

Serves 4

When cooking shrimp, very little water is needed. Basically, you're steaming the shrimp. Even without Gullah Seasoning, this is how you boil shrimp.

-Charlotte

Place the water, wine, Gullah Seafood Seasoning and bay leaf in a large heavy-bottomed pot and bring to a boil. Add the red pepper flakes. Bring back to a boil. Add the shrimp and simmer for 5 to 6 minutes, or until the shrimp turn pink and are firm to the touch. Adjust seasonings to your taste.

Serve with cocktail sauce. Garnish with lemon.

1 cup water

1/2 cup white wine

4 tablespoons Gullah Seafood Seasoning (see page 82)

1 bay leaf

2 pounds large (21/25 count) unpeeled shrimp

Red pepper flakes to taste

The Chicken Lady, 1994 © Jonathan Green

Gullah
SOUP & STEWS

Cabbage Soup

She-Crab Soup – "Gullah Style"

Chicken Soup

Fresh Vegetable Soup

Red Bean Soup

Fish Head Stew

Neck Bone Stew

Frogmore Stew

Catfish Stew

Chicken Stew

Conch Stew

Awendaw Shellfish Stew

Oxtail Stew

Chicken Flock, 1994 © Jonathan Green

SOUPS & STEWS

My great-grandfather was the local preacher. In my early years, I was listening to him. The local preacher preaches when the regular preacher is spread between several churches. Every other Sunday, when the local preacher preached, the people didn't hardly give money. His collection would be a dollar and a quarter total. My great-grandfather would bring a couple others with him to my grandmama's. I was a grown man before I knew a chicken had legs and thighs. She cooked three or four chickens, but there are fourteen people she's got to feed plus those three visitors. The children got the chicken neck or the back or the wings. Or we ate it in soup. The preacher got the best. ... I saw one local preacher put a drumstick in his pocket. I realized then preachers can be just like anybody else.

– Frank

2 smoked turkey necks or large beef bones

3 quarts water

1 cup peeled and diced rutabaga

1 cup diced onion

1 clove garlic, minced

1 cup chopped peeled carrots

2 cups seeded and diced tomatoes

1 cup diced celery

1 teaspoon sugar

1 teaspoon dried basil

2 cups chopped cabbage

1 1/2 teaspoons salt

1/4 teaspoon black pepper

1 tablespoon Gullah Seasoning (see page 79)

Cabbage Soup
Serves 4 to 6

Put the turkey necks and water in a stockpot and bring to a boil. Skim off foam. Reduce to a brisk simmer for 45 minutes, continuing to skim off any foam.

Add the rutabagas, bring to a boil, reduce heat and briskly simmer for 10 minutes. Add the onions, garlic, carrots, tomatoes, celery, sugar and basil, and stir to combine. Briskly simmer for 20 minutes, or until the vegetables become tender.

Add the cabbage, salt and pepper and briskly simmer for 25 minutes, or until the cabbage is tender but not mushy.

Stir in the Gullah Seasoning and serve.

She-Crab Soup – "Gullah Style"

Serves 4

She-Crab Gullah style: that's basically milk and crab meat. Sometimes I will make a roux. I cook it until it smells like hazelnut and I know then it's time to add the milk. The original recipe was done by William Deas, a butler for one of the old Charleston families and the chef at Everett's restaurant. He used crab roe (the eggs) but I don't. Some don't like the texture or look of the eggs. The sherry is optional. I use plenty.

-**Charlotte**

Stick the cloves in the onion. Place the onion, celery, milk and mace in a heavy-bottomed pot. Bring to a low boil, reduce to a simmer and simmer until the onion is soft, about 30 minutes. Strain the milk and reserve. Discard the solids.

Melt the butter in a heavy-bottomed pot. Whisk in the flour. Cook over medium heat, whisking occasionally, for 5 minutes. Whisk in the hot milk. Add the Gullah Seafood Seasoning and briskly simmer, whisking occasionally, for 3 to 5 minutes, or until the liquid thickens. Simmer for an additional 10 minutes, whisking occasionally. Add the crabmeat and sherry, if using, and heat through.

Ladle into serving dishes, garnish with nutmeg and serve.

5 cloves

1 large white onion, peeled and quartered

1 rib celery, chopped

6 cups milk

1/4 teaspoon mace

4 ounces unsalted butter

1/2 cup all-purpose flour

1/4 teaspoon Gullah Seafood Seasoning (see page 82)

1 cup lump crabmeat

1/2 teaspoon dry sherry (optional)

Nutmeg to sprinkle over top when serving

1 (3-pound) whole chicken

1 1/2 gallons water

2 cups diced onion

2 cups diced celery

1 tablespoon chopped garlic

2 tablespoons salt

1/4 teaspoon black pepper

1/4 cup all-purpose flour

1 cup sliced peeled carrots

Chicken Soup

Serves 6 to 8

In the old days, we'd take a yard chicken, usually an old rooster, put it on all day, pull the meat off the bones and that's it. Mama thought the broth had healing qualities so that was also our medicine.

-Charlotte

Place the chicken and water in a stockpot. Add half of the onions, celery and garlic, the salt and pepper. Bring to a low boil, reduce to a brisk simmer, and briskly simmer for 2 hours, skimming off foam. Remove the chicken from the stockpot and let cool. Strain the stock and reserve. Discard the vegetables. Once the chicken is cool enough to handle, remove the skin and meat from the bones and reserve. Discard the bones and any sinew. Cut up the meat.

Rinse the stockpot. Fry the chicken skins in the stockpot to render the fat. Remove the skins and discard, keeping the fat in the pot. Add the remaining half of the onion, celery and garlic and the carrots and sauté them in the rendered chicken fat for about 10 minutes, or until the vegetables are tender.

Stir in the flour and cook for 5 minutes, stirring occasionally to prevent lumps. Stir in the stock and briskly simmer for 10 minutes, or until stock is slightly thickened. Add the chicken to the stock and vegetables in the stockpot and simmer for 5 minutes to heat through.

If adding dumplings, simmer for an additional 5 to 6 minutes after adding, or until the dumplings are firm.

Fresh Vegetable Soup

Serves 4 to 6

Melt the butter. Add onions, celery and garlic and sauté for about 6 minutes, or until tender. Stir in flour and cook for 5 minutes, stirring occasionally to prevent lumps. Gradually stir in the water. Add the carrots, turnips, cauliflower, potatoes and bay leaf. Bring to a boil, reduce heat and briskly simmer for 20 minutes, or until the vegetables are tender. Add the salt, pepper and green peas.

Briskly simmer for 10 minutes for fresh peas, 5 minutes for frozen peas, or until the peas are tender.

1 1/2 ounces unsalted butter

1 cup diced onions

1 cup diced celery

1 clove garlic, minced

3 tablespoons all-purpose flour

2 quarts water

1 cup diced peeled carrots

1/2 cup diced peeled turnips

1/2 cup cauliflower florets

2 cups diced peeled red potatoes

1 bay leaf

2 tablespoons salt

1 tablespoon black pepper

1/2 cup fresh or frozen green peas

1 pound dried red beans

1/2 pound picnic ham, chopped

2 quarts water

1/2 cup chopped onion

1/2 cup chopped celery

1 teaspoon dried thyme

1 teaspoon chopped fresh parsley

1/4 cup canned tomatoes

Pinch sugar

Salt and black pepper

Red Bean Soup

Serves 4 to 6

Wash the beans and soak them overnight. Drain.

Put ham and water in a stockpot. Bring to a boil, reduce heat and briskly simmer for 30 minutes. Add beans, onion, celery, thyme, parsley, tomatoes, sugar, and a dash of salt and pepper. Briskly simmer for 1 to 1 1/2 hours, stirring occasionally, or until the beans are soft. Adjust seasoning as desired.

Fish Head Stew

Serves 4 to 6

You get vitamins from the eye. But take the fish eye out after it's cooked, so you don't serve with the eye looking back.

–Charlotte

Place the fish heads, stock, onion, celery and bay leaves in a large stockpot. Briskly simmer for approximately 1 hour, skimming off foam. The meat on the fish heads should be tender enough to be almost falling off of the bone. Strain and reserve the stock. Remove the meat from the fish heads. Discard the bones, skin, onion, celery and bay leaves.

Heat the oil in a large heavy-bottomed pot. Add the bell pepper and sauté for 4 minutes, or until tender. Add the reserved fish stock, diced tomatoes, tomato sauce, potatoes, basil, oregano and sugar and mix well. Bring to a boil, reduce heat and briskly simmer, stirring occasionally for 20 to 25 minutes, or until the potatoes yield when pierced with a fork. Add the meat from the fish heads and simmer for an additional 15 minutes. Add the Gullah Seasoning and cayenne pepper. Season with salt and pepper as desired.

Mix well and serve.

2 pounds fish heads, preferably grouper

2 quarts fish stock (see page 83)

1 cup diced onion

1 cup diced celery

2 bay leaves

1 tablespoon vegetable oil

1 cup diced green bell pepper

2 cups chopped canned tomatoes

2 cups tomato sauce

2 cups diced peeled white potatoes

2 tablespoons dried basil

1/4 teaspoon dried oregano

1/4 teaspoon sugar

1 tablespoon Gullah Seafood Seasoning (see page 82)

1/4 teaspoon cayenne pepper

Salt and black pepper

3 tablespoons vegetable oil

2 pounds fresh turkey neck bones

All-purpose flour

1 cup diced onion

1/2 cup sliced celery

3 tablespoons all-purpose flour

2 quarts water

1 cup chopped canned tomatoes

Salt and black pepper

Neck Bone Stew

Serves 4 to 6

Back in the old days, fresh neck bone sold at ten to twenty-five cents a pound. Like hogs feet, it was the cheap cut. Nothing's cheap now except fish heads. You can still get those for free sometimes.

-**Charlotte**

Heat the vegetable oil in a pot. Season the neck bones with salt and pepper and flour them. Heat the oil in a heavy-bottomed pot. Working in batches, brown the neck bones on all sides in the oil. Remove the neck bones and set aside. Add the onion, celery and 3 tablespoons of flour, and stir for 5 minutes. Return the neck bones to the pot. Add the water and tomatoes. Bring to a boil, reduce to a brisk simmer, cover, and briskly simmer, stirring occasionally, for 2 hours, or until the meat is tender and easily pulls away from the bones.

Season with salt and pepper as desired and serve.

Awendaw Shellfish Stew

Serves 6 as main course

Heat the olive oil in a heavy-bottomed pot. Add the onion, green pepper, celery and bay leaf and sauté for 10 minutes, or until the vegetables are tender. Add the garlic and sauté for an additional 2 minutes. Stir in the flour and cook for 5 minutes. Stir in the tomato juice and the fish stock and briskly simmer for 5 minutes, stirring frequently to prevent lumps from forming.

Add the Gullah Seafood Seasoning and the crabs and briskly simmer for 15 minutes. Add the clams and briskly simmer until they open. Add the mussels, shrimp and scallops and continue to briskly simmer for 5 to 10 minutes, or until the mussels are open, the shrimp are pink and firm to the touch, and the scallops are tender. Do not overcook.

Remove the backs from the crabs and reserve the shells for deviled crab. Clean out any roe and remove the gills. Crack the crabs in half. Divide the stew between 6 warmed bowls. Add one half of a blue crab to each serving.

1/4 cup olive oil

1 cup chopped onion

1 cup chopped green bell pepper

1 cup chopped celery

1 bay leaf

1 clove garlic, chopped

1/4 cup all-purpose flour

2 cups tomato juice

4 cups fish stock
(see page 83)

2 tablespoons Gullah Seafood Seasoning
(see page 82)

3 whole blue crabs

12 mussels

12 little neck clams

1 pound medium (31/35 count) shrimp

1 pound bay scallops

Oxtail Stew

Serves 4

3 pounds large meaty oxtails, cut in 2 1/2-inch pieces

Salt and black pepper

1 tablespoon dried thyme

2 to 2 1/2 gallons beef or brown stock (see page 85)

1 cup diced onion

1 clove garlic, chopped

1/2 cup diced celery

1/2 cup diced green bell pepper

1/2 cup chopped scallions

1/2 cup diced peeled carrots

2 bay leaves

1/4 cup all-purpose flour

1/4 cup water

Sprinkle the oxtails with salt, pepper and thyme. Place them in a heavy-bottomed pot with the beef stock. Bring to a boil, reduce to a brisk simmer, cover and briskly simmer for 4 hours, stirring occasionally and adding additional stock if needed. Add onions, garlic, celery, green peppers, scallions, carrots and bay leaves, cover and briskly simmer for an additional hour. Whisk the flour into the water in a small bowl. Stir it into the pot. Briskly simmer for an additional hour, or until the sauce has thickened and oxtails are fork tender and almost falling off the bone.

Adjust the seasoning as desired. Remove the bay leaves and serve.

The Prescott Farm, 1994 © Jonathan Green

Gullah
MEATS

Pot Roast

Stuffed Pork Chops with Apple-Raisin Stuffing

Roasted Chicken

Marinated Chicken

Roasted Leg of Lamb

Country Ham with Gravy

Fried Chicken – "Gullah Style"

Pigs' Feet

MEATS

When I was a child, we had a rooster named Broke Mouth. He had an accident with his beak. One short, one long. He was our pet. We raised chickens. Broke Mouth lasted a while. I don't remember whether he got slaughtered or not. Probably so. But he came back, in a way, fifty years later. This lady from Parks and Recreations, she and I got in a conversation. I was talking about yard chickens. She says, "I'm going to bring you one. You can roast it, smother it in gravy or whatever you want." She brought this rooster and he was so beautiful. I said, "I can't cook him." My brother says, "I'll kill him for you." I say, "No!" We had him in a cage for a little while. Then we started letting him out and he stayed on the rail of the deck in front of the restaurant. We named him Gullah Ro. The customers loved him. He would mosey up just before we opened the door at 11 o'clock and he'd be peeking in the door. He'd hang around on the deck and peer at customers. He'd have his picture taken. We had him more than a year. Such a beautiful rooster and so sweet. One day he just up and left us.

– Charlotte

5 pound boneless chuck roast

Salt and black pepper

1 clove garlic, finely minced

1/4 cup all-purpose flour

1 cup chopped onion

4 tablespoons vegetable oil

8 to 10 cups beef or brown stock (see page 85)

Pot Roast

Serves 6 to 8

Sprinkle the roast with salt and pepper. Rub it with the minced garlic and flour it. Heat the oil in a heavy-bottomed skillet and brown the meat on both sides, about 10 minutes. Add the beef stock and bring it to a brisk simmer. Cover the skillet tightly with aluminum foil. Briskly simmer the roast and stock for 2 hours, or until the roast is tender. Check occasionally and add additional stock if necessary.

If desired, add chopped onion, carrots, celery and peeled red potatoes 30 minutes before the roast is done. Continue the brisk simmer until the vegetables are tender, removing the roast to a 200-degree oven to keep it warm if it should be ready before the vegetables.

Serve the vegetables on a platter with the roast and the juices from the roasting pan.

Stuffed Pork Chops With Apple-Raisin Stuffing

Serves 4

Preheat oven to 350 degrees. Make pockets in the chops by cutting a slit in the center of fat side and cutting a pocket toward the bone. (You could have this done at the meat counter.) Sprinkle the chops on both sides with Gullah Seasoning for Baking and Roasting.

Combine the bread, apple, celery, onions, raisins, sage and thyme. Add half of the chicken stock and mix well. Fill the pockets with the mixture and close the openings with wooden toothpicks. Place the chops in a roasting pan. Sprinkle with paprika, if desired.

Cover the pan tightly with aluminum foil and bake the chops for 25 minutes. Remove the foil and bake for an additional 20 to 25 minutes, or until the chops are done and the outside edge of the stuffing is nicely browned. The juices should run clear when the chops are pierced with a knife.

Remove the pork chops and keep warm in a 200-degree oven. Place the roasting pan on the top of the stove over medium heat. Add the flour and stir over medium heat for 2 minutes, or until the flour has turned light brown. Stir in the remaining half of the stock and simmer briskly, stirring frequently until the stock thickens, about 5 minutes.

Place the pork chops on a serving platter; pour the sauce over them and serve.

---

4 (1 1/2-inch thick) loin pork chops, about 6 ounces each

1/2 teaspoon Gullah Seasoning for Baking and Roasting (see page 80)

1/2 cup diced toasted bread

1/2 cup minced apple, Red Delicious preferred

1/2 cup minced celery

1 cup minced onion

1/2 cup raisins

1/2 tablespoon dried sage

1/2 tablespoon dried thyme

2 cups chicken stock (see page 84)

2 tablespoons all-purpose flour

Paprika optional for color

Roasted Chicken
Serves 4

3 1/2 to 4 pound chicken

1 tablespoon salt

1/4 teaspoon black pepper

1 tablespoon granulated garlic

1 tablespoon dried thyme

1/4 teaspoon ground ginger

Pinch paprika

Butcher's twine

Preheat oven to 375 degrees.

Remove the innards from the cavity of the chicken and rinse the chicken well. Mix the salt, pepper, garlic, thyme and ginger and rub the mixture onto the chicken. Sprinkle the chicken with paprika. Tie the legs together at the ends of the drumsticks with butcher's twine. Place the chicken in a roaster, cover tightly with aluminum foil, and roast for 30 minutes. Remove the foil and roast for an additional hour, basting occasionally with the juices in the roaster. The chicken is done when the internal temperature of the breast is 165 degrees and the juices run clear when the thigh is pierced with a fork.

Remove the chicken and let rest for at least 10 minutes before carving to allow the juices to settle. Garnish with parsley if desired.

Marinated Chicken

Serves 6 to 8

Heat the olive oil in a sauté pan. Add the bell pepper, onion and garlic and sauté for 3 minutes, or until tender. Add the white vinegar, apple cider vinegar and bay leaf and simmer for 15 minutes. Add the lemon juice. Cool. Put the chicken breasts and marinade in a sealed bag and refrigerate for at least 1 hour or overnight. Turn over occasionally.

When ready to cook, drain off the marinade and season the breasts with salt and pepper. Heat a grill pan over medium-high heat. Working in batches, cook the meat in the grill pan for about 5 minutes per side, or until the breasts are firm to the touch and the juices run clear when the chicken is pierced with a fork. Serve.

1/4 cup olive oil

1/2 cup finely chopped red bell pepper

1/2 cup finely chopped onion

1 clove garlic, chopped

1/4 cup white vinegar

1/4 cup apple cider vinegar

1 bay leaf

1 teaspoon fresh lemon juice

6 to 8 boneless, skinless chicken breasts, about 3 pounds

Salt and black pepper

Roasted Leg Of Lamb

Serves 6 to 8

---

5 pound leg of lamb, shank half

Salt and black pepper

1 clove garlic, sliced

1/4 cup olive oil

2 teaspoons chopped fresh parsley

2 teaspoons finely chopped fresh rosemary

1/2 cup sliced carrots

1/2 cup chopped onion

1/2 cup chopped celery

4 cups beef or brown stock (see page 85)

We never got a lamb when I was a child. That came later in life. We'd do lamb on Christmas. Mama had the dinner and I'd do the lamb. The secret is fresh garlic and low heat.

-Charlotte

Preheat oven to 400 degrees.

Sprinkle the lamb with salt and pepper. Make three to four slits on top of lamb and insert a slice of garlic in each slit. Mix the olive oil, parsley and rosemary. Rub it over the entire lamb. Place the carrots, onion and celery in a roasting pan.

Place the lamb on top of the vegetables. Roast for approximately 2 1/2 hours for medium rare. A meat thermometer should register 145 degrees. Remove the lamb from the oven and allow to rest for 10 minutes before slicing.

To make *au jus* to serve with the lamb, remove the lamb from the roasting pan. Add the beef stock to the pan. Scraping the bottom of the pan to bring up any drippings, bring the juices and stock to a boil. Strain if desired.

Serve with the sliced lamb.

Country Ham With Gravy

Serves 4

Use red-eye gravy with country ham. The red eye is adding a touch of coffee to the mix. I guess it keeps your eyes open. A Southern thing.

-Charlotte

Heat the oil in a skillet until hot but not smoking. Add the ham and fry for about 4 minutes on each side. Remove the ham and set aside. Add the onions, garlic and pepper to the skillet and sauté for 5 minutes, or until the onions are tender. Add the flour and stir over medium heat for 5 minutes, or until the flour has turned light brown. Stir in the chicken stock, bring to a boil, reduce heat and briskly simmer, stirring frequently for about 10 minutes, or until the liquid thickens. Stir in the coffee and briskly simmer for 5 minutes, stirring frequently.

Return the ham to the skillet and simmer for 5 minutes. Adjust the seasoning, if desired. Adjust the consistency by adding a little more chicken stock if it is too thick.

Serve over grits or grits spoon bread.

2 tablespoons vegetable oil

4 (1/4-inch thick) slices country ham, about 1/2 pound

1/4 cup chopped onion

Dash granulated garlic

Dash black pepper

1/4 cup all-purpose flour

1 1/2 cups chicken stock (see page 84)

1 cup black coffee

3 pounds cut-up fryer pieces

3 tablespoons Gullah Seasoning for Fried Foods (see page 80)

2 cups all-purpose flour

1/4 teaspoon black pepper

1 quart vegetable oil or lard

Fried Chicken – "Gullah Style"

Serves 4

Season the chicken with half of the Gullah Seasoning for Fried Foods. In a bowl mix the flour, the remaining half of the Gullah Seasoning for Fried Foods and the pepper. Roll the chicken in the flour mixture until covered evenly.

Heat the oil in a deep pot to 375 degrees. Working in batches so as not to crowd the pot, place pieces of the floured chicken into the hot oil. Fry for approximately 15 minutes, or until the chicken floats to the top of the pot and turns golden brown. When the chicken is pierced with a fork, the juices should run clear.

Drain briefly on paper towels and serve.

Pigs' Feet

Serves 8

Pigs' feet. They're also called trotters. When I was a child, Mama cooked pigs' feet, potato salad and collards. That's the meal. With pigs' feet, you need a lot because it's mostly fat. When I eat them I peel off all the skin, get down to where there's gristle and lean meat, eat that and suck the bone. The fat I skip. Some people eat the whole thing.

When he killed a hog, Daddy would take it to a friend's house and smoke it. Thirteen hogs was the most he raised at a time. Daddy would kill three or four during the holidays and share with family members. Butchered them there in the yard. He'd put them in a barrel. We children pulled the hair off. That was fun though. Slush, slush. Slapping the hog. Patting it. That was playing. I was nine or ten then. Every part of that hog was going to be used. They say everything but the squeal, and that's the truth.

-**Charlotte**

Place the pigs' feet in a heavy-bottomed pot and add enough water to cover them. Add the onion, celery, green pepper, garlic, salt and pepper. Bring to a boil, reduce to a brisk simmer, cover, and briskly simmer for 2 hours, or until the pigs' feet are tender. Skim off any foam that rises to the top while cooking.

Add the tomato sauce, hot sauce, ketchup, Worcestershire sauce and vinegar and briskly simmer, covered, for an additional hour, or until the meat begins to fall off of the bones. Serve hot with the sauce.

8 pigs' feet

1 cup chopped onion

1 cup chopped celery

1 cup chopped green bell pepper

1 clove garlic, chopped

1/2 teaspoon salt

1/2 teaspoon black pepper

2 cups tomato sauce

1/2 teaspoon hot sauce, Texas Pete preferred

1/4 cup ketchup

1/4 cup Worcestershire sauce

1 tablespoon white vinegar

Lowcountry Hunter, 1986 © Jonathan Green

Gullah
GAME

Baked Quail

Venison Burgers

Venison Stew

Fried Turkey

Wild Rabbit Stew

Holiday Preparation, 1988 © Jonathan Green

GAME

My father wasn't a hunter. His friends hunted and shared with him. In exchange for venison, he did plumbing work. Marsh hen we had every now and then, but I didn't like the fishy taste. Mama never cooked possum. But raccoon she cooked. I couldn't see myself eating that. The meat is so dark I'd be thinking that could be a dog or a cat. She made sweet potatoes, peeled them, cut them up, put around the raccoon and baked it, but that's not a recipe I'm repeating.

– Charlotte

We had a single-barrel shotgun. And we had dogs for every kind of hunting. A deer dog is born with the scent. They won't track a rabbit or coon. If they do start that, you tie them off 'til they are cured. A deer dog smells from the air. Rabbit dogs smell from the trail. A beagle follows the track even if it's three or four hours old. If you think a deer is in a particular area, you put somebody on the end of a trail. That's the stand. Somebody else takes the dogs into the woods and the hunters wait on the stand. They still do this on Wadmalaw and do the same in Awendaw, which in a lot of ways is the same kind of place. In the old days, you'd skin the deer and cut him up. The meat was kept on ice as long as you could, but most you gave away. People had ice boxes but no freezers. All that running around and hooping and I did manage to shoot one deer. Rabbits, those we shot enough to sell.

Walking By, 2007 © Jonathan Green

We had frog legs, but not from what we called a "bullfrog." It was a "spring chicken." People ate the legs of a bullfrog when they had nothing else. We ate rabbits and coons. I didn't eat possum, others did. We didn't hunt alligators on a regular basis, but if one come around the house, we had to kill him. When I was about fifteen, we killed one that had nineteen metal dog tags in its stomach. He was eight feet long. We shot him twenty-seven times with buck shot. He'd just eaten a dog. The dog's tail was sticking out his mouth. An alligator can outrun a horse in the start. I've seen them go that fast. We had alligator tail occasionally, but we didn't eat the one who'd eaten the dog.

We'd use sling shots to kill birds. A thrasher was the easiest to kill. Sparrows, next. We didn't eat blackbirds because they looked like crows. Robins, those were the fattest. We'd trap the robins – prop up a wire cage with feed inside it, pull the stick out. The best way was to partly fry the bird, then put it in some gravy. Flour, water, salt, pepper, onion. We cooked that ourselves. Killing and cooking birds was a kid's game.

– **Frank**

4 quail (domestic works well)

1/4 teaspoon salt

1/4 teaspoon black pepper

1 tablespoon minced garlic

1/2 cup chopped onion

4 slices bacon

2 ounces unsalted butter

2 tablespoons all-purpose flour

Baked Quail

Serves 4

Preheat oven to 350 degrees

Season the quail with salt, pepper and garlic. Place in a roasting pan, lay bacon on top of quail and cover the pan tightly with aluminum foil. Bake for 45 minutes, or until the juices run clear when a thigh is pierced with a fork. Remove the quail from the roasting pan and reserve the pan juices.

Warm the butter in a small sauté pan over medium heat. Stir in the flour and cook for 2 minutes, stirring constantly. Add the onions and continue to stir over medium heat for an additional 10 minutes, or until the flour turns light brown. Stir in the pan juices and bring to a boil. Place the quail in a 6 1/2 x 12 x 2-inch baking dish. Pour the sauce over the quail. Return the quail to the oven and bake for an additional 10 minutes, or until the quail and sauce are thoroughly heated. Serve.

Red Fish, 1998 © Jonathan Green

Gullah
SEAFOOD

Baked Stuffed Flounder

Salmon Patties

Barbecued Shrimp

Garlic Shrimp

Shrimp with Hominy

Deviled Crabs

Soft-Shelled Crabs

Crab Cakes

Garlic Crab

Seafood Casserole

Catfish Cakes

SEAFOOD

Even though our house was only a mile from the saltwater boat landing, we girls were not allowed there. That was a no-no. But every now and then we'd sneak off and go crabbing and fishing. The boys could go, but none of them worked in the creek. Still, seafood was always coming into the house. Locally, there were people who made a living on the water and they'd come by the house with shrimp, oysters, crabs and conchs. Mullet, catfish, whiting, spot, croaker were the fish. Not much flounder. In the latter day, when I was sixteen or so, we ate shark and stingray wings. I've seen the machines for punching scallops out of those wings. Why? My mama used to make a nice stew out of skate wings. You peel the wing and scrape it. You use boiling water because the skin is very tough. She'd also fry skate wings. I loved that because the little sinews became crisp. But, you know, people are afraid of something that looks different. They won't eat it.

-Charlotte

We lived right by the creek and learned to swim at an early age. We could take a rowboat and go twenty yards to cast for shrimp and mullet. When the tide was low, they stayed right there in a hole. We'd catch a washtub full, forty quarts of shrimp, a hundred or so mullet. But I had to clean or head them. Castnets were made of cotton. I still have an uncle on the island who can knit a net.

At high tide, we'd go out on in the bateau to go hand-lining – that's a cotton line wrapped around a stick with a sinker on the end and two hooks. I was sixteen before I saw a rod and reel. By then we were used to hand lines. If you're good enough, you could throw it out thirty feet. With big yachts going to Florida in the Intracoastal Waterway, we'd get big waves, and if our little boat was loaded with shrimp or fish, that mattered. But we knew how to swim, and we knew to take care of each other. We caught stingray and saved the wings. The stinger could kill you or make you wish you were dead. We'd take the knife and cut off the skate wings, throw the other back. Spot-tailed bass we caught. At high tide the shrimp go in the marsh to feed and the bass follow them. For the bass, we had a cotton gill-net. For gill nets, some used wire fence, but that chicken wire was stiff, so a fish could work his way out or under. Still, without the money, we'd use anything at hand to net a fish.

> I was sixteen before I saw a rod and reel. By then we were used to hand lines. If you're good enough, you could throw it out thirty feet.   -Frank

Women from Saint Helena, 1998 © Jonathan Green

For shark we had to go to the channel. I was around eight or nine when we started that. It was dangerous but we liked the excitement, and we didn't go for the really big sharks. We had a small boat. We had those same hand-lines with a mullet or a shrimp for bait. Four or five of us in the boat, so you put a shark in there too, you got to beat him. One time we beat a hole in the bottom of the boat and had to row back quick. Another time we just plain couldn't get back. We lost one of the two paddles. We tried for an hour. Then an old man rowing came and got us. I guess we could have gotten over to Edisto Island. The channel is about a mile wide, and halfway in the middle was where the sharks were.

Until the 1970s, we had boat builders on the island. They used cypress because it didn't rot. I remember they used water to shape the wood, soaked the planks to bend them for the pointed bow. These were flat bottom, two-seat bateaus, twelve to fourteen feet long. Two oar locks. Outboard motors didn't arrive in our neighborhood until the late sixties. Usually two people rowed. The crabbers and oystermen had boats up to sixteen foot, so they could carry more.

Besides rowing, we could scull with one oar in the back. We did that for floundering at night. A guy in the front shines the kerosene lantern. Flounders eyes would show and then you stick them in the head with a gig. Flashlights were a big step up. We used a house lantern in the beginning – an oil lamp turned up high – not a Coleman lantern. But floundering was at night and not so popular. Casting for shrimp was better at night too, but most did it in the day. If they worked in Charleston, they'd go in the creek at night for food.

Crabs like the mud. They lay in gutters and settle in the mud when the tide goes down, so we'd bog for them. Five or six years old, we'd walk along, see a ripple in the mud, and there's the crab. You put a stick on him to hold him steady. Soft shell we'd get with a net, but there's only a short season for those.

Some days we'd cut school, get a bushel of oysters and cook 'em, wait for the chickens to lay eggs, boil the eggs, and have a little party. Oysters and eggs. Then there was cooter soup. My grandmother made it. That's the saltwater turtle, a terrapin. Turtle's got some good meat. This was in the early days. They said it was bad luck, and my grandmother stopped.

-Frank

Baked Stuffed Flounder

Serves 4

1 1/2 ounces unsalted butter

1/2 cup chopped onion

1/2 cup chopped celery

1 egg, lightly beaten

1/4 teaspoon cayenne pepper

1/2 teaspoon Gullah Seafood Seasoning (see page 82)

1/2 cup fresh claw crabmeat, gently picked over for shell and cartilage

8 (4 - 6 ounce) flounder fillets, skinless

Salt and black pepper

2 tablespoons fresh lemon juice

Paprika

Preheat oven to 350 degrees

Heat the butter in a skillet. Add the onion and celery and sauté for 3 minutes, or until tender. Cool. Combine the egg, the onion and celery mixture, the cayenne pepper and Gullah Seafood Seasoning. Fold in the crabmeat.

Sprinkle all the fillets with salt and pepper. Place 4 of the fillets in a greased baking pan. Spread out 2 tablespoons of the crab mixture on each of the 4 fillets.

Place the remaining 4 fillets on top. Sprinkle with the lemon juice. Sprinkle with paprika. Bake for 20 minutes, or until the flesh of the fish is opaque and flakes easily.

Serve immediately.

Salmon Patties

Makes 6 patties

Combine the egg, onions, peppers, Gullah Seafood Seasoning, mayonnaise and flour. Mix well. If using canned salmon, check for any skin, bones and cartilage and remove, and drain off juice. Flake the fresh salmon. Combine with the other ingredients. Divide into 6 patties.

Heat the oil in a skillet to 375 degrees. Fry the patties for about 5 minutes per side, or until golden brown on both sides.

Drain on paper towels and serve.

1 egg, lightly beaten

1/4 cup chopped onion

1/4 cup chopped green bell pepper

1 tablespoon Gullah Seafood Seasoning (see page 82)

2 tablespoons mayonnaise

1/4 cup all-purpose flour

16 ounce can of salmon or 1 pound of cooked fresh salmon, bones and skin removed

1 cup vegetable oil

1 cup tomato sauce

1/2 cup Worcestershire sauce

1/4 cup fresh lemon juice

1/4 cup fish stock
(see page 83)

4 tablespoons minced garlic

1 tablespoon white vinegar

1 teaspoon olive oil

3 tablespoons light brown sugar

1 tablespoon chili powder

2 teaspoons dry mustard

1 bay leaf

1 pound medium
(31/35-count) shrimp,
peeled and deveined.

Metal or wood skewers

If using wood skewers, they must be soaked in water for 30 minutes before use to prevent them from burning.

Barbecued Shrimp

Serves 4

Peel shrimp and then barbecue, or barbecue with the shell on. I do it both ways. If you keep the shell on, when you peel it to eat, the sauce gets on your fingers and back on the shrimp.

-Charlotte

Combine all the ingredients, except the shrimp, in a saucepan and bring the mixture to a boil for 5 minutes, stirring frequently. Cool to room temperature. Put the shrimp in a container and pour the sauce over the shrimp. Cover and refrigerate for 3 1/2 hours, turning once halfway through. When ready to cook, drain the shrimp and put 3 or 4 on each skewer.

Heat a grill pan over medium heat. Cook the skewered shrimp in the grill pan for 3 to 5 minutes per side, or until the shrimp are pink and firm to the touch. Serve hot.

ON COOKING SHRIMP

When I was growing up we cooked shrimp by dropping them in the boiling water and leaving them four or five minutes. Heads on was best and sometimes we'd cook them right on the bank using saltwater from the creek and even added seaweed for taste. Take them out when they're pink, or drain the water off and they're ready to serve.

-Frank

Garlic Shrimp

Serves 4

My mama cooked with a lot of garlic. My grandmama grew wild garlic in her garden. Garlic was also a tea to cure colds. She'd put the garlic in a jar with vinegar for that.

-**Charlotte**

Heat the olive oil in a skillet. Add the garlic and sauté for 2 minutes. Add the shrimp and sauté for 1 minute. Add the lemon juice, sherry and paprika and sauté, stirring frequently, for 3 minutes, or until shrimp are pink and firm to the touch.

Season with salt and pepper, stir in parsley, and serve immediately.

4 tablespoons olive oil

4 cloves garlic, crushed

1 pound medium (31/35-count) shrimp, peeled and deveined

2 tablespoons fresh lemon juice

2 tablespoons dry sherry

1 teaspoon paprika

Salt and black pepper

1 tablespoon chopped fresh parsley

5 cups water

1 1/4 teaspoons salt

1 1/3 cups stone-ground grits

1 1/2 ounces unsalted butter

1/2 cup chopped onions

1/4 cup all-purpose flour

1 pound large (21/25-count) shrimp, peeled and deveined

1 1/2 cups fish stock (see page 83)

1 tablespoon Gullah Seafood Seasoning (see page 82)

Shrimp With Hominy

Serves 4

We grew up on shrimp and brown gravy. Brown the flour and oil until you get the color you want, then add the liquid. It's a *roux* in New Orleans. An equal amount of fat to flour.

-Charlotte

For the grits: Put the water and salt in a pot and bring to a boil. Add the grits, stirring constantly to avoid lumps. Simmer, stirring occasionally, for 40 to 45 minutes, or until the grits are tender.

For the shrimp: Heat the butter in a skillet. Add the onions and sauté for 5 minutes or until tender. Stir in the flour and continue to cook over medium heat, stirring constantly for about 5 minutes, or until the flour has turned light brown. Stir in the Gullah Seafood Seasoning and fish stock and cook, stirring occasionally, for another 5 minutes or until the sauce begins to thicken. Add the shrimp and cook for 5 minutes, or until it is pink in color and firm to the touch.

Serve over the grits.

Seafood Casserole

Serves 4

Use 8 x 8-inch casserole dish or 3 (8-ounce) oval casserole dishes. Preheat an oven to 325 degrees.

Heat the butter in a skillet. Working in batches, sauté the shrimp and scallops gently in the butter for about 3 minutes, or until firm. Remove them from the skillet with a slotted spoon and set them aside to cool.

Combine the shrimp, scallops, crabmeat, Swiss cheese and Cheddar cheese in a bowl and mix thoroughly. Place the mixture in the casserole dish(es). Pour the white sauce over the seafood mixture. Bake for 25 minutes, or until the cheese has melted and the casserole is hot through.

Remove from oven and let stand for 5 minutes before serving.

2 ounces unsalted butter

16 large (21/25-count) shrimp, peeled and deveined

1 pound bay scallops

8 ounces claw crab meat, gently picked over for shell and cartilage

4 ounces Swiss cheese, grated

2 ounces sharp Cheddar cheese, grated

2 cups white sauce (see page 86). *Best if made just before the casserole and kept at room temperature.*

1 ounce unsalted butter

8 ounces skinless catfish fillets

1 (approximately 8-ounce) russet potato, boiled, peeled, then mashed

1/2 cup finely chopped onion

1/4 cup minced celery

1 clove garlic, minced

1/2 teaspoon Tabasco sauce

1 tablespoon dry mustard

1/4 teaspoon dried thyme

2 tablespoons salt

1/4 teaspoon black pepper

3 eggs

1 cup vegetable oil

Catfish Cakes

Makes 6 cakes

Heat the butter in a large skillet. Working in batches, sauté the catfish in the butter for 10 minutes, or until the flesh is opaque and can be easily flaked. Remove from the skillet and cool. Once cool, flake the fish.

Put the catfish, mashed potatoes, onion, celery, garlic, Tabasco, mustard, thyme, salt and pepper in a bowl. Beat the eggs, add to the mixture and combine well. Divide the mixture into 6 cakes. Heat the oil in a skillet. Working in batches, sauté the cakes for about 5 minutes on each side, or until browned and firm to the touch. Drain on paper towels and keep warm in a 200-degree oven until all the catfish cakes have been cooked. Serve.

Autumn Winds, 2001 © Jonathan Green

Gullah
VEGETABLES & SIDES

Fried Okra

Okra Gumbo

Collard Greens with Ham Hocks

String Beans

Rutabaga

Southern-style Lima Beans

Black Beans

Succotash

Candied Sweet Potatoes

Baked Macaroni & Cheese

Apple Salad

Potato Salad

Pinto Bean Pie

VEGETABLES & SIDES

Not too far from the water we had a farm my father used to plant. He grew watermelons, beans, field peas, "ice" potatoes, okra. Ice potatoes are the little red ones. For ourselves, we did okra, sweet corn, cibby beans. My mom made a great dish with that – beans, okra and peas cooked together. We planted sweet potato. When we harvested them, we dug a bank, lined the hole with straw and then buried them. That took us through the winter. Sweet potato was our school lunch. Sometimes we had a hoe cake or the ice potato stewed in a little bacon fat.

There was a big white farm nearby where we'd pick cotton. I hated cotton. That was the money for school. Hard on your hands, both cotton and okra. Okra gives you burns and a rash. I was never a good farmer; that's why I learned to cook. The most cotton I picked was a full sack, but once you pressed it down you had a half a sack. I wouldn't push mine down. "What's wrong with yours?" Daddy would say. This was picking at the Hale Farm. We set out tomatoes for the farmer. Then we did strawberries. I had a problem with that too. Picking beans thirty-five cents a crate, but the crate had to be full. Me, it would be half a crate. Picking okra turned me into a cook.

– Charlotte

1/2 cup milk

1 cup all-purpose flour

1 cup yellow cornmeal

1 tablespoon Gullah
Seasoning for Fried Foods
(see page 80)

1 cup vegetable oil

1 pound fresh or frozen
okra, sliced into thick rounds

Fried Okra

Serves 4

Okra with rice. Doesn't get more Gullah than that. Okra comes from Africa. Rice was grown there, too. Sauté your okra and add after the rice has cooked. You sauté to keep the okra from getting slimy. The secret to breaded okra is to have it a little wet so the breading clings. Then add a little seasoning, salt and pepper, and deep-fry it. We grew up with fried okra, not breaded, but sautéed with the butts meat, ham or bacon. That, served with white rice nice and dry, and sometimes add a little shrimp. Perfect. A Gullah feast.

-Charlotte

Combine the milk, flour, cornmeal and Gullah Seasoning for Fried Foods to make a thick batter.

Heat the oil in a skillet to 375 degrees. Working in batches, dip the okra slices in the batter and fry for 4 to 5 minutes or until crisped golden brown. Drain on paper towels. Serve immediately.

Okra Gumbo

Serves 4 to 6

Place the ham and water in a heavy-bottomed pot and bring to a boil. Add the onion, garlic, green pepper, bay leaf and tomato sauce and briskly simmer for 10 minutes. Add the okra, return to a brisk simmer and briskly simmer for 1 hour, stirring occasionally, or until the okra has fallen apart. Add the sausage and chicken and briskly simmer for 15 minutes. Add the red pepper flakes, Gullah Seafood Seasoning and shrimp and briskly simmer until the shrimp turn pink and are firm to the touch, about 5 minutes. Remove the bay leaf. Serve over rice.

1 cup diced cooked picnic ham

5 cups water

1 cup chopped onion

1 clove garlic, chopped

1 cup chopped green bell pepper

1 bay leaf

4 cups tomato sauce

1 pound fresh or frozen sliced okra

1/2 cup diced smoked sausage

1/2 cup diced cooked chicken

1/2 teaspoon red pepper flakes

1 teaspoon Gullah Seafood Seasoning (see page 82)

20 medium (31/35 count) shrimp, peeled and deveined

1 pound smoked ham hocks

6 quarts water

2 pounds collard greens

1 teaspoon sugar

1 teaspoon red pepper flakes

Salt and black pepper

Collard Greens With Ham Hocks

Serves 6

There was a time I couldn't have imagined cooking collards without the ham hocks. I can now. Sometimes I just steam the collards, saute some onions and add those – that's the health-food way. You can also cook them in chicken or beef broth. Vegetable broth works too. A lot of people don't eat pork in any form. I sometimes cook them with smoked turkey wings. A traditional meal would be collards, macaroni and cheese, and fried chicken.

-Charlotte

Put the ham hocks and water in a stockpot and bring to a boil. Reduce to a brisk simmer, cover and briskly simmer for 2 1/2 hours, or until the ham hocks are tender. Wash the collard greens and cut the leaves off of the stalks. Place the leaves in cold water and sprinkle with salt to wash out any sand. Wash thoroughly three times, the third without salt. Cut the leaves into thirds.

Remove the cooked ham hocks from the pot. Place the collards in the pot with the ham hock broth. Sprinkle with the sugar. Place the ham hocks on top of the collards. Bring to a boil, reduce to a brisk simmer, cover and briskly simmer for 55 minutes. Add the red pepper flakes. Continue to briskly simmer for an additional 5 minutes, or until tender.

Serve the greens by themselves or with the hocks and some of the cooking liquid from the pot, which is known as "pot likker."

String Beans

Serves 6 to 8

I remember Mama and my grandmama sitting on the porch snapping beans. My uncle John used to plant all kinds of things. Corn, lima beans, peas. When my father got up in years and wasn't making much farming, he gave that up and did only plumbing. My uncle kept farming. Every night we'd shell the beans and take those to the market in town. Cibby beans, the green limas. My mom used to do the green lima, put in a little vinegar, cook until almost done, take the whole baby okra and lay it on top. That's a good addition to Sunday dinner.

-Charlotte

Put the ham and water in a pot, bring to a boil, reduce the heat and briskly simmer for 30 minutes. Add the beans, salt and pepper. Cover and briskly simmer for 20 minutes, or until the beans are tender. Do not overcook. Remove from the heat and let stand for 5 minutes to allow the flavors to meld. Adjust the seasonings as desired.

1/2 pound cooked picnic ham, finely diced

2 quarts water

2 pounds string beans, tips and tails removed

1 tablespoon salt

1/3 teaspoon black pepper

1 cup diced picnic ham

1/4 pound smoked turkey neck bones

6 cups water

3 cups peeled and cubed rutabaga

1/4 teaspoon sugar

1/3 teaspoon salt

1/3 teaspoon black pepper

Rutabaga

Serves 2

Put the ham, bones and water in a heavy-bottomed pot. Boil for 25 minutes. Add the rutabaga, sugar, salt and pepper. Bring to a boil, reduce the heat and briskly simmer for 30 minutes, or until the rutabaga is tender. Remove bones and discard. Serve immediately.

1 pound dried lima beans

1/2 pound smoked ham hocks

1/2 pound fresh or smoked pig's tail

4 quarts water

1 tablespoon granulated garlic

1 teaspoon salt

1 teaspoon black pepper

2 cups chopped onion

Southern-Style Lima Beans

Serves 4

Wash the lima beans and soak them in warm water for 1 hour. Drain.

Put the ham hocks, pig's tail, water, garlic, salt and pepper in a stockpot. Bring to a boil, reduce to a brisk simmer. Cover and briskly simmer for 45 minutes. Add the lima beans, onion and a dash of salt and pepper. Bring to a brisk simmer. Cover and briskly simmer, stirring occasionally for 45 minutes to 1 hour, or until the beans are soft. Adjust the seasoning as desired. Serve with white rice or alone as a side dish.

Black Beans

Serves 4

Black bean is also called a turtle bean. In a field they'd be mixed in with other crops. We'd pull them out to cook.

-Charlotte

Wash the beans and soak them in warm water for 2 hours. Drain.

Put the ham hocks and water in a stockpot. Bring to a boil, reduce to a brisk simmer and cover. Briskly simmer for 1 hour. Add the beans and onion. Bring to a boil, reduce to a brisk simmer, cover and briskly simmer for 35 minutes. Add the scallions, stir to combine, and continue to simmer for an additional 5 minutes, or until the beans are soft. Season as desired with salt and pepper. Serve with sour cream.

1 pound dried black beans or turtle beans

1/2 pound smoked ham hocks

3 quarts water

1 cup chopped onion

1/2 cup chopped scallions

Salt and black pepper

Sour cream for garnish

Succotash

Serves 4

Put the butter beans and chicken stock in a heavy-bottomed saucepan. Bring to a boil, reduce to a brisk simmer, cover and briskly simmer for 35 minutes for fresh butter beans or 20 minutes for frozen, or until the butter beans are tender. Stir occasionally. Add the corn and butter. Simmer for 5 minutes, or until the corn is tender. Season as desired with salt and pepper.

1 1/2 cups fresh or frozen baby butter beans

3 cups chicken stock (see page 84)

1 1/2 cups corn, cut fresh from cob or frozen

3/4 ounce unsalted butter

Salt and black pepper

4 pounds sweet potatoes, washed and pierced several times with a knife to prevent bursting

4 ounces unsalted butter, melted

2 1/2 cups light brown sugar

1 tablespoon cinnamon

1 tablespoon allspice
1/4 cup water

2 tablespoons fresh lemon juice

Candied Sweet Potatoes

Serves 8 to 10

Long ago we'd pull the sweet potato out the bank, the dirt teepee where they were stored. We'd peel it and fry it. Now we fancy it up a little. Add some vanilla and a little sugar.

-Charlotte

Put the sweet potatoes in a heavy-bottomed pot, cover them with water, and boil for approximately 25 minutes, until they yield when pressed lightly with a fork. Remove the sweet potatoes from the water and let cool.

Preheat an oven to 350 degrees. Peel the cooled sweet potatoes and cut them into 1/2-inch slices. Place potatoes in a single layer in a 13 x 9 inch baking dish.

Mix the remaining ingredients together in a bowl and pour over the sweet potatoes. Bake for 35 minutes, stirring occasionally to ensure that the sweet potatoes cook evenly. They should be soft but not mushy when done. The butter and brown sugar mixture should form a thick sauce.

Baked Macaroni & Cheese

Serves 4 to 6

A lot of people say macaroni and cheese is not Gullah, but my grand-mama made it. She'd add green peppers she'd grown. The peppers were like jalapenos or Spanish peppers. They were so hot you couldn't eat much. Left more for the people who like hot. Macaroni and cheese is a Sunday meal.

-Charlotte

Preheat oven to 375 degrees.

Cook the macaroni in salted water until just tender. Drain and reserve. Whisk together the melted butter, evaporated milk, whole milk, eggs, mustard, salt and pepper. Add macaroni to the mixture. Add the diced Cheddar and 2 cups of the grated Cheddar. Pour the mixture into a greased 9 x 5 x 2.75 inch pan. Sprinkle with the remaining 1/2 cup of the grated Cheddar and then with the paprika. Bake for 20 minutes, or until top is brown and the macaroni and cheese is firm to the touch.

8 ounces elbow macaroni

4 ounces unsalted butter, melted

1 cup evaporated milk

1 cup whole milk

3 eggs, lightly beaten

1 teaspoon prepared mustard

1/4 teaspoon salt

1/4 teaspoon black pepper

1 cup finely diced sharp Cheddar cheese

2 1/2 cups grated sharp Cheddar cheese, divided

Pinch paprika

Apple Salad

Serves 4

3 cups diced apples, Red Delicious usually, but it's your preference

1 tablespoon fresh lemon juice

1 cup diced celery

1/2 cup chopped walnuts

1/2 cup raisins

3 tablespoons mayonnaise, Hellmann's® preferred

4 large lettuce leaves

Toss the apples and lemon juice in a bowl. Add the celery, walnuts, raisins and mayonnaise and toss to combine. Place the mixture on the lettuce leaves and serve.

Potato Salad

Serves 6

3 pounds red potatoes

1/2 cup chopped green bell pepper

1/2 cup chopped celery

1 cup diced sweet pickles

1/4 cup mayonnaise, Hellmann's® preferred

1 teaspoon prepared mustard

1 teaspoon salt

1/2 teaspoon black pepper

4 boiled eggs, peeled and finely chopped

Pinch paprika

Peel the potatoes, cut in cubes, and cook in salted water until tender, about 25 minutes. Drain and cool. Combine the potatoes, green peppers, celery, pickles, mayonnaise, mustard, salt and black pepper. Fold in the eggs.

Add salt and pepper as desired. Sprinkle with paprika. Cover and refrigerate for 3 hours to let flavors meld.

Pinto Bean Pie

Makes 2 (9-inch) pies

Preheat oven to 350 degrees.

Combine all of the ingredients except the pie shells and pecans in one bowl. Mix thoroughly. Purée in a food processor. Divide the mixture between the pie shells.

Top with the chopped pecans. Bake for 45 minutes, or until firm.

1 packed cup dark brown sugar

1 cup granulated sugar

4 eggs, lightly beaten

2 cups cooked pinto beans, mashed, then puréed in the food processor

1 cup milk

1 tablespoon pure vanilla extract

4 ounces unsalted butter, melted

2 unbaked 9-inch pie shells

1 cup chopped pecans

Harvest Festival, 2001 © Jonathan Green

Gullah
RICE DISHES

Vegetarian Field Peas & Rice

Gullah Cuisine's Famous "Gullah Rice"

Mama Julia's Sunday Red Rice

Lemon Rice

Dirty Rice

Hoppin' John

Oyster Pilau

Herring Pilau

Okra Pilau

RICE DISHES

My mama's style was definitely Gullah. She spoke with an accent, but not as thick as some others. She moved to Charleston from McClellanville when she was young. She was living at Anson Street, stayed a while and got married. They moved to Do As You Choose Alley up not too far from Morris Street. She had a first-born son and a daughter there. My father said if we're having a lot of kids we need to be in the country. He asked his momma for an acre of land in Ten Mile. That's when he built the house on Gadsenville Road.

He really was a self-made man. He taught himself how to build houses and to be a plumber. Up in Awendaw, he put in baths for a lot of people. Father would get water. He'd find water. Drove wells with no real tools. He drove them with a homemade rig, a sledge hammer and a block of oak. But plumbing and carpentry was a side line. He worked at the cotton press on Charlotte Street and commuted to Charleston. The farming was done early in the morning before going to work. When he came home and on weekends, he did that and the houses. His salary was close to nothing, and he had a lot of kids to feed.

Father plowed with a horse we called Red. Father never got a tractor. He didn't grow a whole lot of cotton. Several of them would put their cotton together. Took it to the gin and divided what they were paid. Rice he didn't plant, but would get from others. I remember trying to get all the husks off. The cracked rice! Oh my, that was hard to deal with. We had a wooden mortar, like in the old photographs. Brown rice. When I think about Gullah rice, it's got all that behind it.

– Charlotte

Vegetarian Field Peas And Rice

Serves 10

2 cups dried field peas

2 quarts water

2 tablespoons minced garlic

1 tablespoon vegetable oil

1 bay leaf

2 tablespoons minced fresh cilantro

2 tablespoons chopped fresh parsley

Salt and black pepper

1 cup chopped onion

1/2 cup chopped scallions

1 cup chopped canned tomatoes

2 teaspoons dried thyme

3 1/2 cups raw converted rice, Uncle Ben's® preferred

Wash the peas and soak in warm water for 1 hour. Drain. Put the peas, water and garlic in a stock pot. Bring to a boil, reduce heat and briskly simmer for 40 minutes. Stir in the bay leaf, cilantro and parsley, a dash of salt and pepper, the onion, scallions, tomatoes and thyme. Cover and briskly simmer for 10 minutes, or until the peas are tender. Stir in the rice, bring to a simmer, cover and simmer for 20 to 25 minutes, or until the rice is tender.

Season as desired and remove the bay leaf. Fluff with a fork and serve.

Gullah Cuisine's Famous "Gullah Rice"

Serves 6 to 8

Heat 1/4 cup of the oil in a heavy-bottomed pot. Season the chicken with the Gullah Seasoning. Working in batches, brown the chicken in the oil. Remove the chicken from the pot and set aside. Add the onions and sauté for 5 minutes, or until they are tender. Drain off the excess fat.

Return the chicken to the pot. Add the chicken stock. Bring it to a boil, reduce heat and briskly simmer for approximately 15 minutes, or until the juices run clear when the chicken is pierced with a fork. Remove the chicken and set aside. Drain the stock and discard the onions. Return the stock to the pot.

Heat the butter in a heavy-bottomed pot over medium heat. Whisk in the flour and cook it over medium heat, whisking for about 10 minutes, or until the flour turns dark brown. Whisk this into the stock, then bring it to a boil. Reduce heat and briskly simmer for approximately 5 minutes, or until the stock thickens. Add the rice, bring to a simmer. Cover and simmer for 20 to 25 minutes, or until the rice is tender.

While the rice is cooking, remove the meat from the bones. Discard the bones, skin and any sinew. Dice the meat.

In a separate heavy-bottomed pot, heat the remaining 1/4 cup of the vegetable oil. Add the peppers and carrots and sauté for 5 minutes, or until the vegetable are tender. Add the shrimp and sauté for 3 minutes. Add the chicken and sausage and heat through. Add all to the rice, mix and cook until thoroughly incorporated and heated through. Serve.

1/2 cup vegetable oil, divided

1 1/2 pounds chicken pieces

3 tablespoons Gullah Seasoning (see page 79)

1 cup finely diced onion

5 cups chicken stock (see page 84)

4 ounces unsalted butter

1/4 cup all-purpose flour

2 cups raw converted white rice, Uncle Ben's preferred

1/2 cup finely diced green bell peppers

1/2 cup finely diced peeled carrots

1/4 cup medium (31/35-count) shrimp, peeled and deveined

1/4 cup sliced Andouille sausage

4 thick slices bacon

2 thick slices picnic ham, chopped

1/2 cup chopped onion

1/2 cup chopped green bell pepper

1/4 cup chopped celery

1 clove garlic, chopped

2 cups tomato sauce

2 1/2 cups water

1 tablespoon dried basil

1 bay leaf

1/4 teaspoon sugar

2 cups raw converted rice, Uncle Ben's® preferred

Salt and black pepper

Mama Julia's Sunday Red Rice

Serves 6

Even when I was grown and married, those Sunday family dinners were so important to me. In the old days, we went into the fields and picked the overripe tomatoes so we could make tomato sauce. The Gullah way is the no waste way. Peel them, mash them and let them cook. Or use the bought sauce. Take rice and add onion and green pepper, sauté that with a little bacon. That's red rice. Of course, there are different versions of red rice now. Add sausage or shrimp.

-Charlotte

Fry the bacon in a heavy-bottomed pot to render the fat. Remove the bacon and reserve it for another use. Sauté the ham, onion, peppers and celery in the rendered bacon fat for 5 minutes, or until the vegetables are tender.

Add the tomato sauce, water, basil, bay leaf and sugar. Stir to combine and bring to a boil. Add the rice, bring to a simmer, cover, and simmer for 20 to 25 minutes, or until the rice is tender.

Remove the bay leaf. Adjust the seasoning with salt and pepper as desired. Fluff with a fork and serve.

Okra Pilau

Serves 6 to 8

Fry the bacon and ham in a heavy-bottomed pot until brown, about 10 minutes. Add the onions and granulated garlic, stir, and sauté for 5 minutes, or until the onions are tender. Add the okra and sauté for 10 minutes if fresh and 5 minutes if frozen. Remove the okra mixture and reserve.

Add the stock to the pot and bring to a boil. Add the rice, salt and pepper and simmer. Cover and simmer for 20 to 25 minutes, or until the rice is tender. Add the okra mixture, incorporate thoroughly, and heat through.

Fluff with a fork and serve.

3 slices bacon, chopped

1/2 cup chopped picnic ham

1/2 cup chopped onion

1 teaspoon granulated garlic

2 cups fresh or frozen sliced okra

4 cups chicken stock (see page 84)

2 cups raw converted rice, Uncle Ben's preferred

1 teaspoon salt

1 teaspoon black pepper

Harvest Eve, 2000 © Jonathan Green

Gullah
QUICK BREADS

Buttermilk Biscuits

Corn Muffins

Dumplings

Hoe Cakes

Grits Spoon Bread

ON QUICK BREADS

When my mama started up, a biscuit was flour and some shortening. With time, we started doing different things. Mama skimmed off the top of the milk and put that in the biscuit, so that made buttermilk biscuits. Do you judge a Southern cook just by her biscuits? Well some people just can't do biscuits. Biscuits are not easy. When I was young, I remember doing biscuits pretty good. For a long stretch I didn't do them and when it was time to go back, they never came out as before. I played with it and played with and every now and then I will hit and make a biscuit that melts in your mouth. Some people have a knack for it, perfect every time. I mean you can always eat mine and someone will say it's good, but I'll know it's not. Kind of like wine tasting. That's the level you judge biscuits on. *The Washington Post* was impressed by mine. "Light, flaky and served piping hot, with a generous pat of butter." That's their description.

– **Charlotte**

Gullah DESSERTS

Pie Crust

Mama Julia's Apple Pie

Sweet Potato Pie

Pecan Pie

Bread Pudding with Hard Sauce

Peach Cobbler

Sweet Potato Soufflé

ON PECANS

My grandmother planted cotton. She did a little farming even in her eighties. She had a problem with her legs, so she'd sit in a chair and hoe. She lived to ninety-three. She sold her stuff down at the market. My grandmama spoke Gullah, the kind you can't understand. My grandmama's terminology: "Bitals" was food. Bitals. "Homney" was hominy. "Pick up me some homney," she'd say, "E done dis." She'd use "e" or "him" for everybody. "Him done gone. Him been her. Him ain't want nothing t' eat." She would also say, "honna" for listen. "Honna chilrun." As in, "Honna chilrun, stay from 'neath the pecan tree." Eating the pecans was a no no. She used to sell them in the market in town. We'd help her pick them up. After she had enough for the market, then she would let you help yourself. Then you could eat pecan pie.

-**Charlotte**

Pie Crust

For 1 (9-inch) pie crust

1 1/4 cups all-purpose flour

1/2 teaspoon salt

1/2 cup shortening

1/4 cup ice water

Place the flour in a bowl. Add the salt and mix well. Add the shortening, cutting it in with a pastry cutter or two knives until the shortening is blended in and the mixture resembles coarse meal.

Sprinkle in the ice water and toss to mix. Gently form the dough together with your hands and pat it into a 6-inch disk. Wrap in plastic wrap and refrigerate for 2 hours or overnight.

Unwrap the refrigerated disk and place it on a lightly floured board. Place the rolling pin in the middle of the disk and roll forward. Bring it back to the center of the disk and roll backward.

Turn the disk 45 degrees, checking to be sure that it is not sticking. Continue to gently roll the crust in this manner, taking care not to roll the edges too thin, until you roll out a circle larger than the outside rim of the 9-inch pie plate so that you can have an edge to crimp up. Lay the dough inside the pie plate and refrigerate it while you make the filling.

Mama Julia's Apple Pie

Makes 1 (9-inch) pie

This recipe is named for my mother. This is her recipe. She was famous for her apple pie. Try this recipe and you'll see why.

-**Charlotte**

Preheat oven to 350 degrees.

Cook the apples in a pot with the butter, sugar, cinnamon, allspice and lemon zest for 5 minutes, or until the apples start to soften and become translucent. Cool.

Make an egg wash by whisking together the egg, water and salt. Line a 9-inch pie plate with one of the crusts. Spoon in the cooled apples.

Roll out the remaining dough and gently drape it over the apples. Seal the edge with egg wash and crimp it. Brush the top with egg wash. Cut several slits in the top to let out the steam that will result as the pie bakes.

Place the pie on a baking sheet and bake, turning back to front midway through, for approximately 40 minutes, or until the top crust is an even golden brown. If the edges darken too soon, cover them with a strip of aluminum foil.

2 (9-inch) pie crusts (preceding page)

5 Granny Smith apples (about 3 pounds), peeled, cored and thickly sliced

3 ounces unsalted butter

1/2 packed cup light brown sugar

1 tablespoon cinnamon

1 tablespoon allspice

Zest of 1 lemon

1 egg, lightly beaten

1 tablespoon water

Pinch salt

1 (9-inch) pie crust
(see page 191)

6 pounds sweet potatoes,
washed and pierced with a
knife to prevent bursting

2 eggs, lightly beaten

2 tablespoons pure vanilla
extract

1 teaspoon fresh lemon juice

1 teaspoon fresh orange zest

1/4 cup all-purpose flour

1 1/3 cups granulated sugar

3 tablespoons light brown
sugar

3 tablespoons cinnamon

1 tablespoon nutmeg

1 tablespoon allspice

1 tablespoon cardamom

Sweet Potato Pie

Makes 1 (9-inch) pie

Put the sweet potatoes in a heavy-bottomed pot, cover them with water and boil for approximately 25 minutes, or until they yield when pressed lightly with a fork. Remove from the water and let cool. Once cool, peel the sweet potatoes.

Preheat oven to 350 degrees.

Mash the cooled sweet potatoes. Beat together the potatoes, eggs, vanilla, lemon juice and orange zest. Combine the flour, two sugars and the spices, and beat into the potatoes. The mixture should be uniform with no lumps. Spoon into the pie crust.

Bake for 45 minutes, or until the crust is golden brown and the filling is firm.

Pecan Pie

Makes 1 (9-inch) pie

I don't remember my mama making pecan pie. She made homemade pecan cake. My sister who died, she could make that same pound cake with pecans. Since she died, I can't bring myself to use that recipe. But this pie will melt in your mouth.

-**Charlotte**

Preheat oven to 400 degrees.

In a bowl, mix the eggs, sugar, corn syrup, cider vinegar, vanilla, butter and salt. Pour the mixture into the unbaked pie shell. Add the pecans. Bake the pie for 35 minutes, or until the pecans have risen to the top and the pie is firm to the touch. Let set 10 minutes before cutting.

1 (9-inch) pie crust
(see page 191)

3 eggs, lightly beaten

3/4 packed cup dark brown sugar

1/2 cup dark corn syrup

1 tablespoon cider vinegar

1 teaspoon pure vanilla extract

1 ounce unsalted butter, melted

Pinch salt

1 cup coarsely chopped pecans

1 cup pecans halves

Bread Pudding With Hard Sauce

Serves 4 to 6

1 cup granulated sugar

1 packed cup light brown sugar

1 cup milk

3 eggs, lightly beaten

1 tablespoon ground cardamom

1/2 tablespoon cinnamon

10 slices day-old bread, torn in pieces

1 ounce unsalted butter, melted

1/2 cup drained sliced canned peaches

1/4 cup raisins

Bread pudding was Mama's dessert, but I didn't like those cooked raisins she had in there. She would take all the stale bread and put it in a big dish pan, put sugar and evaporated milk on it. I'd eat that part. I loved that raw part. In Gullah cooking nothing goes to waste. Even now in the restaurant nothing goes to waste. I use the overripe tomatoes in my okra soup. Day-old bread goes in the pudding.

-Charlotte

Preheat oven to 350 degrees

Whisk together both sugars, the milk, eggs, cardamom and cinnamon. Add the bread, melted butter, peaches and raisins. Stir just to combine.

Pour into a greased 9 x 5 x 2.75-inch baking dish. Bake for 45 minutes, or until firm. Let cool for 10 minutes before putting on hard sauce.

Hard Sauce

2 pasteurized egg whites*

1 cup powdered sugar

1 teaspoon pure vanilla extract

1 1/2 ounces unsalted butter, melted

Beat the egg whites with an electric mixer until they are fluffy. Beat in the sugar, vanilla and butter for 3 minutes.

Spread over warm bread pudding.

*Pasteurized eggs in the shell are available in some markets or use a liquid or frozen egg product.

1 (9-inch) pie crust (see page 191)

4 cups canned sliced peaches, drained and syrup reserved

2 tablespoons cornstarch

1/1/4 cups granulated sugar

1/2 packed cup dark brown sugar

1/4 teaspoon allspice

1/4 teaspoon cardamom

1/4 teaspoon cinnamon

1/2 teaspoon pure vanilla extract

Peach Cobbler

Makes 1 (9-inch) pie

Back in the days, everybody had a peach tree in the yard, but they weren't the rosy peaches like we get in the store. They never got ripe. When my brother lost his son around the time of Hurricane Hugo in 1989, he planted a peach tree in his memory. That tree grew real peaches, and I thought about all those years we made do with little knotty peaches.

-Charlotte

Preheat oven to 375 degrees.

Mix the cornstarch with 3 tablespoons of the peach syrup and reserve. Combine the granulated sugar, brown sugar, allspice, cardamom, cinnamon and vanilla. Add the peaches and mix well. Pour into a greased 8 x 8 baking dish. Cover with the pie crust. Crimp the edges if desired. Bake the cobbler on an aluminum foil-lined baking sheet for 35 to 40 minutes, or until the crust is golden brown. Let stand 10 minutes before serving.

Sweet Potato Soufflé

Serves 6

Preheat oven to 350 degrees.

Combine all main ingredients, and pour into a greased 9 x 5 x 2.75-inch casserole dish.

For the topping, mix the butter and flour together in a bowl with a pastry blender or two forks until a course texture is obtained. Add the sugar and nuts, and mix.

Spread on top of sweet potato mixture. Bake in the preheated 350 degree oven for 35 to 40 minutes, or until the top is brown and the soufflé is firm to the touch.

Main ingredients:

3 cups cooked mashed sweet potatoes, about 2 pounds raw

4 ounces unsalted butter, softened

1 1/2 cups sugar

2 eggs, lightly beaten

1 teaspoon pure vanilla extract

1 teaspoon cinnamon

1 teaspoon ground cardamom

Topping:

2 ounces unsalted butter, softened

1 cup all-purpose flour

1/2 packed cup light brown sugar

1 cup chopped pecans

Contemplation, 1999 © Jonathan Green

Gullah
BEVERAGES

Eggnog

Comfort Tea

Iced Tea

Fresh-Squeezed Lemonade

Kesha's Sweetgrass Wedding Punch

1 quart milk

6 eggs, lightly beaten

1/4 cup sugar

1 teaspoon pure vanilla extract

1 teaspoon nutmeg

Eggnog
Serves 8

Heat the milk in a heavy-bottomed saucepan until scalding hot. Remove 2 cups. Whisk together the eggs and sugar in a bowl. Gradually whisk in the 2 cups of hot milk.

Whisk this egg mixture into the remaining milk in the saucepan and stir it over low heat until the mixture is thick enough to coat a spoon, about 15 minutes. Add the vanilla and nutmeg. Pour into a heatproof container.

Cool to room temperature, cover and refrigerate for 3 hours. Serve.

3 cups milk

4 whole cardamom pods

1 large tea bag

Sugar as desired

Comfort Tea
Makes 3 cups

We had a lot of teas in the old days. Mint tea. Catnip tea. Milk and hot tea served at night. When I left home and met different people, that's when I picked up comfort tea. Maybe at home we had comfort enough. …
-Charlotte

Put the milk and cardamom pods in a heavy-bottomed saucepan and heat to a bare simmer for 10 minutes. Add the tea bag and return to a bare simmer for 10 minutes. Remove cardamom and tea bag. Add sugar as desired. Serve hot.

Iced Tea

Makes 3 ½ quarts

In heavy-bottomed saucepan, bring 2 quarts of the water to a boil. Remove the saucepan from the heat, add the tea bags, and let them steep for 4 minutes.

Remove the tea bags, add the sugar and the remaining water. Stir to dissolve the sugar.

Cool to room temperature. Add more sugar to taste if desired. Serve in glasses over ice.

3 ½ quarts water

12 family-size (.55 oz.) tea bags

1 cup sugar

10 lemons

2 ½ quarts water

1 cup sugar

Fresh-Squeezed Lemonade

Makes 2 ½ quarts

Slice the lemons in half and squeeze out the juice. Strain to remove seeds and set aside. In a heavy-bottomed saucepan, simmer the lemons, sugar and half of the water on medium heat for 3 minutes, or until sugar is dissolved. Remove the lemons and strain. Stir in the reserved lemon juice and the remaining water. Add more sugar to taste if desired. Chill. Serve in glasses over ice.

Kesha's Sweetgrass Wedding Punch

Makes 5 gallons

Slice the lemons in half and squeeze out the juice. Strain to remove seeds and set aside. In a large pot, put 1 gallon of the water and the sugar. Simmer over medium heat for 3 minutes, or until sugar dissolves. Remove from the heat, add the reserved lemon juice, remaining water, Kool-Aid®, moonshine, and pineapple juice and mix well. Chill.

Serve in glasses over ice.

6 lemons

4 gallons water

4 cups sugar

19 ounce can Kool-Aid®
(flavor of your choice)

1 quart moonshine or corn
liquor

3 quarts pineapple juice

Distant Thoughts, 2002 © Jonathan Green

Chapter Four

IN CLOSING

FRANK: IN CLOSING

I can't say I married Charlotte because she was a good cook. I married her because she is a pretty lady and we just happened to be compatible. She just happened to be a very good cook. Courting, I did try cooking for her. I cooked a steak ,which she said was, "tough." Once back in Mount Pleasant, Charlotte was working for her brother at the paint and body shop. She wanted to return to school – Johnson & Wales cooking school. By the time she got her degree, I was getting out of the fire department, so we started a catering business. We got a job with a big company up in Dorchester. Ten different caterers were interviewed and we were picked. Breakfast, lunch and dinner for a hundred people six months out of the year. Grueling. We had a good staff but Charlotte and I did most of the cooking. That gave us the start in the restaurant. It taught us good lessons, taught us to trust what we knew.

My grandfather was saying, "If you don't have your own property, you don't have anything. God bless the child who has his own."

I was always regimental. My whole life, everything I did was team oriented. Football, Army, United Parcel. I even took the New York policeman test but I'd just gotten married and Charlotte didn't want me to do that. I went to the parcel service in New York for 13 years. Then I came back to Mount Pleasant and joined the fire department. At the time, we had one girl. We wanted more. I couldn't see raising children in New York. Where we lived in the Bronx, I saw little kids so corrupted. Kids ten years old would be out on the street at two o'clock at night. I had a real good job, but raising the child meant more to me than a good job. So we came back. Life around Charleston was far from perfect, but Charlotte and I had had something good here and we wanted that for our children.

My grandfather, though he didn't join the church until he was older, was more of a Christian than most who went to church. He was a very thoughtful fellow and gave a lot to people. Basically, he taught me the value of having your own. Most of the people on the island were working for somebody, a job in the city or working on other farms. He said if you don't have your own, people can take whatever you got at any time. One guy bought a mule and didn't have a farm. They took the mule back because he couldn't pay for it. My grandfather was saying, "If you don't have your own property, you don't have anything. God bless the child who has his own. Whatever you do, buy property." The kids he raised did it. Some even went back to Hart Plantation. I'd like to go live back there myself in a little bitty house, one with no stairs. I'll talk Charlotte into that.

CHARLOTTE: IN CLOSING

I didn't go to college when I got out of high school. I went to a trade school and took courses to be a medical assistant. Got certified. I worked in a hospital in New York. I was in New York in the late sixties. I didn't cook up there for a living, but I did a lot of entertaining. I was exposed to different nationalities. New York was a melting pot. I lived in the Bronx and Manhattan. I was single for a while, but I met Frank and we got married. Our daughter Kesha was born in New York. When she was six we decided to come back here and raise her in the South. After we moved back, we had Katia, our second daughter. We wanted to bring them up with a slower lifestyle. New York was too fast. We didn't see New York as a place to raise children.

When we got here, I went to work for my brother at his auto paint and body shop and worked there for nineteen years. I attended Johnson & Wales in 1988. From Johnson & Wales, I learned sauces. I was raised with gravies. I also learned how to cook in quantity and I learned management – how to operate a restaurant. We started the catering in 1995, and my baby sister Rita was there from the beginning helping out. We started the restaurant in May of 1997. It's a family affair. Rita comes by the restaurant three times a week after work. They call her "Sergeant" because she wants everything looking right and working right. She doesn't tell *me* what to do, but she might give me gentle advice. She's a part of this – it's part of who she is. She likes to see it grow and to speak on it for improvement.

I cook the desserts and I do the meats and the chickens. Rita sometimes helps with the apple pies. She does it just like our mama. It melts in your mouth, it's so good. My daughter Kesha has worked here for six years. She's a good cook, but she mostly handles the business side of things – the catering and banquets.

Family stops by the restaurant all the time. Sometimes we have big gatherings. If a lot of family comes, say twenty or more, we'll eat family style in the Julia room, which was named for my mother. If it gets too busy out in the restaurant, I might need to go out. And if it gets too crazy, my family will pitch in.

In part, I think Gullah cooking is an attitude. My mama cooked for years for a Jewish family over by the Citadel. She learned how to do all the kosher recipes. I can't swear she brought any of that home, but who can say. From way back, Gullah cooks were adopting from Europe, the Caribbean and, of course, from Africa. I've done a little bit of eating in a lot of places. I've never consciously brought a recipe

Family stops by the restaurant all the time. Sometimes we have big gatherings. If a lot of family comes, say twenty or more, we'll eat family style in the Julia room, which was named for my mother.

back, but it's good to go where the natives eat and sample their food. I'm always looking for a Gullah equivalent. Gullah cooking to me is giving food a good flavor.

I've had people come from Japan. One lady said she had to go all the way to Japan just to learn about Gullah Cuisine. She was in Japan watching television and they did something on this restaurant. An actress, a pretty girl, did a scene on the beach here and this went on to include us. This lady saw it over there, so I suppose I can say that Gullah has gone international now.

Mount Pleasant has grown. All around Ten Mile has grown up. Big houses are all through the woods. The new hospital is being built. My brothers were good businessmen. One took a fruit stand on Coleman Boulevard and with his younger brother started a body shop. I started keeping books for them. They purchased this area where the restaurant is, which was then the edge of Mount Pleasant. It was dirt cheap then. My brothers are proud men. Another brother has a floor-sanding company. A top designer called him up to New York just after the inauguration of Barack Obama. My mama pushed them. My father helped too. They were all hard workers. The farming at home gave them a business sense.

Gullah, Gullah, Gullah. You hear the word everywhere these days. I don't know exactly how you would define something that's as big as what is all around you.

My husband is the same. He always had a good job, always worked hard. He came from that farming background and he always did well. When we built our house, we couldn't get insurance because we were outside the Mount Pleasant town limits. Actually the fire truck would have come to us so it was others he worried about. Frank got together with my brother and the preacher and they started the Awendaw Volunteer Fire Department. They got neighbors from all the unincorporated areas to work together. When they needed money, they had fish fries and oyster roasts. He stayed with the Mount Pleasant Fire Department though. When he retired as a captain from that, he started cooking with me. And yes, I taught him everything. And no, he's not a better cook than me. He's good, but I held back from him. I didn't tell him everything. You know, women just throw into the pot; men stop and measure. I don't have to measure. And who wants the cooking to come out the same every time?

Gullah, Gullah, Gullah. You hear the word everywhere these days. I don't know exactly how you would define something that's as big as what is all around you. What I remember best about my mama isn't from my childhood, it's from when I was married and came back from New York. Two and three times a week she had us gather around for meals. To me that was the most sensual experience, that sitting together as a family, sharing whatever was going on in the neighborhood, what was going on in the family. That was a wonderful thing my mother did. She

Charlotte's Mama's Sunday Dinner

Fried Chicken

Red Rice

Macaroni & Cheese

Collard Greens

Okra Soup

Sweet Potato Pie

Iced Tea

prepared food twice, sometimes three times a week. Then every Sunday as well. She made Sunday dinner. That was something special. I went away and came back married with a family and we'd all go over, children and all. It was a chance to be together as a family. She wanted to hold everybody together. Around the dinner table our problems would just smooth out. My mother was the catalyst. She kept us getting along as a family. Those were the days I really enjoyed. The company and the excellent food.

One Sunday afternoon we'd eaten and were sitting around. It was hot that Sunday. We were out on the porch. I noticed she had a different look on her face. I said to my brother, "Mom don't look so good. Something going on." We brought her back inside and asked her how she was feeling. All of sudden something happened. We called the ambulance and when we got into the emergency room, I couldn't understand what she was saying. She was speaking another language. She'd had a stroke. She'd just made dinner. For us, she'd just made dinner.

Recipe Index

Recipe Index

Art and Photography

Listing of paintings by Jonathan Green

All photographs are by Mic Smith except those listed below: